The Trump Teenage Chronicles
Make Adolescence Great Again

By Marc Meyer

2nd Edition
Copyright © 2025 The Marc M. Paper Company, Didcot, Oxfordshire
ISBN 979-8-29616-195-6 ASIN xxx

DISCLAIMER
This is a work of satirical fiction inspired by public figures and events. All characters, situations, and dialogue are products of the author's imagination. Any resemblance to actual persons, living or deceased, or actual events is purely coincidental and intended for humorous purposes only.

This work is not affiliated with, authorized by, or endorsed by Donald Trump, the Trump family, or any Trump-related organizations.

Franklin Delano Roosevelt (the pig) is entirely fictional and not based on any actual presidential pets, living or deceased.
No pigs were harmed in the making of this story. Several fictional tomato gardens may have suffered.

COPYRIGHT NOTICE
All rights reserved. No part of this publication may be reproduced, distributed, or transmitted in any form or by any means without the prior written permission of the author, except for brief quotations in reviews or educational use as permitted by copyright law.
For permissions or inquiries: MarcMPaperCo@proton.me

Your Guide To Greatness

The Garage Sale Empire 5
The Lemonade Corporate Ladder 24
The Pool Party Pyramid..58
The Water Balloon Arms Race 82
The Delivery Service Debacle..104
Independence Day Spectacular 127
The Rehabilitation Campaign 147
The Unlikely Alliance...161
County Fair Comeback 172
Summer's End Summit 198
The Trump Family Halloween Special 217

Foreword

When I set out to write this book, I had no idea it would become a journey into understanding the difference between ambition and friendship, between winning and actually succeeding. The concept had been brewing in my mind for years, this fascination with historical and contemporary figures and what their teenage years might have looked like. There's something irresistible about imagining these larger-than-life personalities as awkward fifteen-year-olds, full of the same overconfidence, spectacular failures, and fumbling toward their eventual destinies that we all experienced.

This is my second work of fiction, following "The Teenage Chronicles of Jesus" (available on Amazon, ASIN B0DT9YBM11), and I'm discovering that there's something deeply entertaining about exploring famous figures through the lens of teenage experience. The idea struck me that every historical figure, no matter how serious or accomplished they became, must have had those formative teenage years filled with embarrassing schemes, social disasters, and the kind of boundless optimism that only adolescence can provide. What if we could capture that raw, unfiltered energy before life taught them restraint?

The satirical concept of teenage Donald Trump had been particularly persistent in my imagination. Here was someone whose adult personality traits are so distinctive and recognizable, what if those same characteristics were already in full force at fifteen? What kind of chaos would ensue? What lessons would be learned? The story that emerged surprised me with its depth, humor, and heart, as supporting characters developed lives of their own and taught both the protagonist and me about what truly matters.

The neighborhoods, schemes, and disasters in this book are entirely fictional, but the emotions are real. Every parent who's watched their teenager launch an overconfident venture, every kid who's learned that friendship matters more than winning, every community that's dealt with one family's enthusiastic chaos, they'll recognize something familiar in these pages. We've all known a teenage version of someone who later became famous, and if we're honest, most of us have been that overconfident teenager ourselves at some point.

My hope is that readers will find themselves laughing not just at the spectacular failures and ambitious schemes, but recognizing the universal journey from adolescent arrogance to genuine wisdom. Because ultimately, this isn't a story about making adolescence great again; it's about discovering that adolescence, with all its confusion and catastrophe, was pretty great all along, especially when it teaches us what friendship really means.

Thanks for reading
Marc

The Garage Sale Empire

The summer of 1962 was supposed to be different. Donald Trump, all fifteen years and three months of him, stood in the driveway of the Trump family house in Jamaica Estates, Queens, wearing his father's navy pinstripe suit, which hung on his lanky frame like a deflated tent, and surveying his empire.

Well, calling it an empire might have been generous. What Donald actually faced was three card tables borrowed from the basement, his mother's old bridge set, and approximately four dozen items that his family had been trying to get rid of for the better part of a decade. But Donald saw potential where others saw problems. It was, he would later tell anyone who would listen, going to be the most tremendous garage sale in the history of Queens. Nobody, and he meant nobody, ran garage sales like Donald Trump.

"Eddie!" Donald called across the lawn to his best friend, Eddie Brickman, who was reluctantly arranging items on the leftmost table. "You're not thinking big enough. This isn't just a garage sale, this is a retail experience."

Eddie looked up from the collection of his mother's old cookbooks and ceramic ashtrays shaped like the state of Florida. "Donald, it's stuff people don't want anymore. You put a price on it, they give you money, they take it home. That's literally what a garage sale is."

"See, that's exactly the kind of small-time thinking that keeps people small-time," Donald said, straightening his father's tie, which reached almost to his knees. "You've got to think customer journey. Brand positioning. Market differentiation. I've been reading my dad's business magazines."

Frankie Malone, whose enthusiasm for Donald's schemes was matched only by his inability to see their inevitable flaws, nearly dropped the box of Christmas decorations he was carrying. "Brand positioning? Donald, that's genius! What's our brand?"

Donald gestured grandly at the modest display. "Premium pre-owned lifestyle solutions. We're not selling used junk, we're selling curated vintage experiences."

"My mom's old blender is a curated vintage experience?" Eddie asked.

"That blender is a classic 1954 Osterizer. Built to last. They don't make them like that anymore. In ten years, people will be paying twice what we're asking just for the nostalgia factor."

Eddie examined the blender, which was missing its top and had a crack running down one side. "Donald, this thing looks like it went through a war."

"Character marks," Donald said without missing a beat. "It tells a story. People love stories."

The morning started promisingly enough. Donald had spent the previous evening making signs with bold black lettering: "TRUMP ESTATE SALE - QUALITY GUARANTEED" and "ABSOLUTELY EVERYTHING MUST GO - PRICES NEGOTIABLE." He'd even convinced his mother to let him use her good tablecloth for the main display table, which he'd positioned to catch the morning sun just right.

Mrs. Henderson from next door was their first customer, arriving at exactly nine o'clock with the dedication of someone who took garage sale shopping seriously. She wore a sun hat, carried a canvas tote bag, and had the focused expression of a general surveying a battlefield.

"Good morning, Mrs. Henderson!" Donald called out, practically bouncing on his heels. "Welcome to what is definitely going to be the best garage sale you've ever experienced. We've got something for everyone, and I personally guarantee that our prices are the most competitive you'll find anywhere in Queens."

Mrs. Henderson nodded politely and began examining the items on the first table. She picked up a ceramic lamp shaped like a pineapple, turned it over to check the price tag, and set it back down.

"That's a genuine 1940s piece," Donald announced, appearing at her elbow with the speed of a seasoned salesman. "My grandmother bought that from a real department store in Manhattan. You're not going to find craftsmanship like that in any of the discount stores."

"It's missing the shade," Mrs. Henderson pointed out.

"Minor detail. Gives you the freedom to customize it exactly how you want. Make it your own. That's actually worth more than having some mass-produced shade that every other person in the neighbourhood might have."

Mrs. Henderson continued her browsing in silence, occasionally picking up items and setting them back down. Donald followed at what he considered a respectful distance, offering running commentary on the provenance and unique qualities of everything she touched.

"Now that," he said when she examined a set of cocktail napkins with faded poodle designs, "those are authentic mid-century modern. My mother got those from Macy's before Macy's became what it is today. People are going to look back on this era as the golden age of American design."

"How much for the napkins?" Mrs. Henderson asked.

Donald consulted his pricing notebook, though he'd memorized every item and price the night before. "I've got those marked at seventy-five cents, but for our very first customer of the day, I could make it fifty cents. That's wholesale pricing. You're practically getting them for what we paid."

Mrs. Henderson handed him two quarters. "I'll take them."

Donald beamed as he made his first sale of the day, carefully writing "SOLD - 50¢" next to "cocktail napkins" in his notebook. This was it. This was how fortunes were built, one satisfied customer at a time.

The next hour brought a steady stream of neighbours and strangers, drawn by Donald's enthusiastic sidewalk advertising and increasingly elaborate sales pitches. He sold a set of mismatched dinner plates to Mr. Kowalski from three houses down ("You can't put a price on conversation starters"), a broken radio to teenage Mary Flynn ("It's got that vintage sound quality that modern electronics just can't replicate"), and a collection of his mother's romance novels to Mrs. Chen ("These are basically American cultural documents").

By eleven o'clock, Donald was feeling invincible. He'd made nearly eight dollars, which was more money than he'd ever had at one time in his entire life. He was beginning to envision expansion opportunities, maybe a weekly garage sale circuit, or perhaps branching into estate sales for other families in the neighbourhood.

That's when the pig arrived.

It started with honking. Not car honking, animal honking. Donald looked up from counting his money to see a small crowd gathering around a battered pickup truck that had pulled up to the curb. In the back of the truck was a wooden crate, and from inside the crate came the unmistakable sound of an extremely unhappy pig.

The driver, a thin man in overalls and a John Deere cap, climbed out and surveyed Donald's garage sale with interest. "You boys running this operation?"

"Yes sir," Donald replied, automatically straightening his father's suit jacket. "I'm Donald Trump, and this is the finest garage sale in Queens. What can I show you today?"

The man nodded toward his truck. "Well, I've got a pig here I need to get rid of. Was supposed to deliver him to a farm upstate, but the farmer backed out last minute. Don't suppose you'd be interested in making a deal?"

Donald's brain immediately began calculating possibilities. A pig was unusual. Unusual was memorable. Memorable was marketable. "What kind of pig are we talking about?"

"Hampshire cross. Young boar, maybe sixty pounds. Smart as a whip and twice as stubborn. Name's Franklin."

"Franklin?" Eddie called over from where he'd been eavesdropping. "Like Franklin Roosevelt?"

"That's right. Franklin Delano Roosevelt, actually. The fellow I bought him from had a sense of humour."

Donald studied the truck, his entrepreneurial instincts tingling. This was clearly an opportunity that a lesser person might miss, but he saw the bigger picture. A pig could be a draw. People loved animals. A garage sale with a pig would be the kind of thing people remembered and told their friends about.

"What would you want for him?" Donald asked.

"Well, I was getting thirty dollars from the farmer. But seeing as you're running a business here and might appreciate the promotional value..." The man paused, sizing up Donald in his oversized suit. "Call it twenty-five dollars."

Twenty-five dollars was more than three times what Donald had made all morning. It was also more money than he actually had. But if there was one thing Donald had learned from reading his father's business magazines, it was that you had to spend money to make money.

"Tell you what," Donald said, channelling every business negotiation he'd ever overheard. "I'll give you fifteen dollars cash right now, plus you can pick out fifteen dollars' worth of premium merchandise from our inventory. That's a thirty-dollar value, and you get the benefit of immediate cash liquidity plus quality goods you can actually use."

The man scratched his chin and looked over the garage sale display. His eyes landed on the pineapple lamp. "That lamp work?"

"Absolutely. Just needs a shade, which gives you creative control over the final aesthetic."

"And that blender?"

Donald glanced at Eddie, who shrugged. "That's a genuine Osterizer. Classic American manufacturing."

"Throw in those golf clubs and you've got a deal."

Donald looked at the golf clubs, which belonged to his father and definitely weren't supposed to be for sale. But this was business, and business required bold decision-making. "Deal."

They shook hands, and within ten minutes, Donald found himself the owner of a sixty-pound pig named Franklin Delano Roosevelt. The pig was currently contained in the same wooden crate he'd arrived in, which the truck driver had helpfully positioned next to the garage sale tables before driving away with fifteen dollars, a lamp, a blender, and Fred Trump's golf clubs.

"Donald," Eddie said quietly, "your dad is going to kill you."

"My dad is going to be impressed," Donald replied, though a small voice in the back of his mind was beginning to question the wisdom of this particular investment. "Do you see any other garage sales in this neighbourhood with a pig? We've just differentiated ourselves from every other amateur operation out here."

Franklin chose that moment to express his opinion about his new circumstances by releasing a sound that was part snort, part squeal, and entirely loud. Several passing pedestrians stopped to see what was happening, which Donald immediately recognized as increased foot traffic.

"Ladies and gentlemen!" Donald called out, climbing onto an overturned milk crate to address the growing crowd. "Welcome to the most unique shopping experience in Queens! Not only do we offer the finest selection of pre-owned household goods, but we're also pleased to present Franklin Roosevelt, the only presidential pig in the tri-state area!"

A little girl tugged on her mother's sleeve. "Mommy, can we see the pig?"

"Of course you can!" Donald announced before the mother could answer. "Franklin here is part of our customer experience program. He's very friendly and loves meeting new people."

This was a complete lie. Donald had no idea whether Franklin was friendly or not. But Franklin seemed to understand that he was being discussed, because he stuck his snout through the slats of the crate and made a softer honking sound that could generously be interpreted as greeting the crowd.

"How much for the pig?" asked a teenager who'd been examining the collection of baseball cards on the middle table.

Donald felt a moment of panic. He hadn't actually intended to sell Franklin, the pig was supposed to be a promotional feature, not merchandise. But the question had been asked publicly, and backing down would look unprofessional.

"Well," Donald said slowly, "Franklin isn't exactly for sale. He's more of a... business partner."

"A business partner?" Eddie whispered. "Donald, what are you talking about?"

"Franklin here is going to be helping us with customer relations and brand management," Donald announced, warming to the idea as he spoke. "He's got natural charisma and genuine appeal. You can't teach that kind of presence."

As if summoned by the compliment, Franklin began working at the latch of his crate with his snout. The wooden box had clearly been designed for transportation rather than long-term containment, and within moments, the latch popped open.

Franklin emerged with the confidence of a politician arriving at a campaign event. He was smaller than Donald had expected but decidedly more dignified. His black and white markings were perfectly symmetrical, and he carried himself with the bearing of an animal who expected to be taken seriously.

The crowd took a collective step backward as Franklin surveyed his new surroundings. Then, with the timing of a natural performer, he trotted directly to the table of baked goods that Mrs. Trump had contributed to the sale and began investigating a plate of yesterday's cookies.

"Franklin!" Donald called out, rushing to intervene. "Those are inventory!"

But Franklin had already selected a chocolate chip cookie and was eating it with obvious satisfaction. The crowd laughed, and Donald realized that people were smiling. Happy customers, he remembered from his father's magazines, were spending customers.

"See that?" Donald announced, turning Franklin's snacking into a selling point. "Even Franklin knows quality when he sees it. Those are genuine homemade cookies, baked fresh yesterday by Mrs. Trump herself. If they're good enough for a discerning pig like Franklin, they're definitely good enough for you."

A woman in the crowd immediately bought the entire plate of cookies. Donald made a mental note to remember this strategy.

The rest of the morning passed in a blur of increasing chaos and surprising success. Franklin appointed himself official greeter, wandering among the customers with the confidence of a seasoned retail professional. He seemed to have an instinctive understanding of customer psychology, staying close to serious browsers, maintaining respectful distance from people who were just looking, and occasionally performing small tricks (sitting on command, shaking hands with his hoof) that kept the crowd entertained.

Donald found himself making sales he never would have made without Franklin's presence. The pig had a way of making people feel comfortable and happy, which translated directly into willingness to purchase questionable merchandise at optimistic prices.

"I've never seen anything like it," said Mrs. Patterson from around the corner, who'd bought a broken jewellery box, three mismatched coffee mugs, and a scarf with a hole in it. "That pig is absolutely charming. Where did you get him?"

"Franklin came to us through a very exclusive acquisition process," Donald replied. "He's not just any pig, he's got genuine personality and natural business instincts. You can't find that combination just anywhere."

By noon, Donald had made forty-three dollars and fifty cents, which was more money than he'd ever imagined possible from one morning's work. More importantly, he'd discovered something profound about the power of unique selling propositions and customer experience differentiation.

The problems started when Franklin decided he was done with customer service for the day.

It began with the Kowalski twins, eight-year-old brothers who'd been taking turns feeding Franklin pieces of a stale coffee cake their mother had bought. Franklin had been patient with their attention for nearly an hour, allowing them to pet his head and scratch behind his ears while their parents browsed the remaining merchandise.

But when the twins decided to see if Franklin could balance a ceramic ashtray on his nose, Franklin's professional demeanour finally cracked.

The ashtray, shaped like the state of Florida and marked at seventy-five cents, sailed through the air and shattered against Mrs. Trump's prized rose bushes. Franklin, apparently satisfied with his editorial comment on the morning's activities, trotted purposefully toward the open garage.

"Franklin!" Donald called out, abandoning his conversation with a potential customer who'd been considering a purchase of three Reader's Digest Condensed Books. "Franklin, we're still working here!"

But Franklin had discovered something far more interesting than customer relations: the family's emergency bag of pig feed that Fred Trump had hastily purchased and stored in the garage after Donald's impulsive morning acquisition.

The next ten minutes involved Donald chasing an increasingly food-motivated pig around the garage while trying to maintain his professional demeanour in front of customers. Franklin, it turned out, was considerably faster and more agile than he looked, and he had the advantage of being closer to the ground and highly motivated by the prospect of premium pig feed.

"Everything's under control!" Donald called out to the growing crowd of spectators. "Franklin's just demonstrating his natural curiosity and intelligence!"

Franklin demonstrated his natural curiosity by knocking over a stack of paint cans, investigating the contents of several cardboard boxes that were definitely not for sale, and somehow managing to open the side door that led from the garage into the house.

"Oh no," Eddie said. "Donald, your mom is going to, "

The sound of crashing dishes from inside the house cut off the rest of Eddie's sentence.

Donald's parents weren't supposed to be home for another two hours. They'd gone to visit Donald's grandmother in Manhattan, leaving him with explicit instructions about which items were and were not authorized for sale. The golf clubs had definitely not been on the approved list, and pigs in the house were so far outside the realm of acceptable behaviour that they'd never been specifically forbidden.

"Ladies and gentlemen," Donald announced to the crowd, which had grown to include several neighbours and at least three people who'd clearly just been walking by and stopped to see what the commotion was about. "We're going to take a brief intermission while Franklin explores our expanded retail space."

More crashing sounds came from inside the house, followed by what sounded suspiciously like his mother's good China hitting the kitchen floor.

"Donald," Eddie said, grabbing his arm. "You have to get him out of there. Right now."

But when Donald tried to follow Franklin into the house, he discovered that the pig had somehow managed to knock over a coat rack, which had fallen against the door and effectively barricaded himself inside. Franklin, meanwhile, had apparently discovered the kitchen and was expressing his appreciation for Mrs. Trump's cooking with a series of satisfied grunts and the occasional crash of falling pots and pans.

"This is fine," Donald told the assembled crowd, though sweat was beginning to show through his father's suit despite the morning air being pleasantly cool. "Franklin's just conducting a quality inspection of our expanded premises. He's very thorough."

A woman in the crowd raised her hand like she was asking a question in school. "Is that pig supposed to be in your kitchen?"

"Franklin operates with a high degree of independence," Donald replied. "That's part of what makes him such an effective business partner. He identifies opportunities that others might miss."

The sound of the refrigerator door opening and closing came from the kitchen, followed by Franklin's enthusiastic honking. Apparently, he'd identified several opportunities in there.

Frankie Malone, who'd been loyally manning the cash box, looked worried. "Donald, maybe we should call someone? Like an adult?"

"Adults don't understand innovation," Donald said, though he was beginning to wonder if innovation was the right word for what was happening. "Franklin's probably just checking our inventory management systems."

A tremendous crash from the kitchen suggested that Franklin had found the inventory management systems lacking.

"Okay," Donald said, making the kind of executive decision that he'd read about in business magazines. "Slight change of plans.

We're going to relocate our operations to the backyard while Franklin completes his inspection."

"Relocate?" Eddie asked. "Donald, we can't move all this stuff. And what about the people who want to buy things?"

Donald looked at the crowd, which had definitely grown larger but seemed more interested in the pig situation than in purchasing pre-owned household goods. Then he looked at the remaining merchandise, which included several heavy items that would be difficult to move quickly. Then he listened to the sounds coming from the kitchen, which suggested that Franklin had discovered the pantry.

"Emergency liquidation sale!" Donald announced. "Everything must go in the next fifteen minutes! Fifty percent off all marked prices!"

This got the crowd's attention. People who'd been browsing casually suddenly became serious shoppers, and Donald found himself making sales faster than he could write them down. Eddie and Frankie grabbed items off the tables and shouted out prices while Donald handled the money and tried to look like he'd planned this whole strategy from the beginning.

In the chaos of the liquidation sale, nobody initially noticed that Franklin had found his way out of the kitchen and was now investigating the backyard. Donald was too busy negotiating the sale of a broken lawn mower to Mrs. Patterson ("It just needs a little mechanical attention, perfect project for someone who appreciates hands-on problem-solving") when Eddie grabbed his arm.

"Donald, look."

Donald looked. Franklin had discovered Mrs. Trump's vegetable garden and was systematically sampling the tomatoes. Not eating them, exactly, but taking a single bite out of each one and then moving on to the next, like a food critic conducting a very thorough tasting.

"He's... methodical," Frankie observed.

"He's destroying my mother's tomatoes," Donald said, feeling the first real panic of the day. The garage sale chaos could be explained away, maybe even spun as entrepreneurial enthusiasm. But destroying his mother's prize-winning tomato plants was the kind of offense that could result in grounding that lasted until school started in September.

Donald climbed over the low fence that separated the driveway from the backyard, his father's suit jacket catching on the chain link and tearing slightly. "Franklin! Franklin, come here, buddy. Let's talk business."

Franklin looked up from his tomato evaluation, a piece of red fruit hanging from his snout, and made a sound that Donald chose to interpret as acknowledgment.

"Listen," Donald said, approaching slowly with his hands visible in what he hoped was a non-threatening gesture. "I understand you're conducting quality control, and I appreciate that level of attention to detail. But maybe we could focus that energy on something that doesn't belong to my mother?"

Franklin considered this proposal while finishing his current tomato. Then he trotted over to the fence that separated the Trump backyard from the Hendersons' property and began investigating their garden as well.

"No, no, no," Donald said, rushing after him. "Franklin, that's expansion into unauthorized territory. We need to stick to our approved operational area."

But Franklin had apparently decided that property lines were merely suggestions. He squeezed under the fence with surprising ease and began exploring the Henderson garden with the same systematic approach he'd applied to the Trumps' tomatoes.

From the other side of the fence came Mrs. Henderson's voice: "WHAT IS THAT PIG DOING IN MY GARDEN?"

Donald climbed over the fence, adding another tear to his father's suit, and found Franklin investigating a row of prize-winning roses. Mrs. Henderson stood in her back door, holding a dish towel and wearing the expression of someone who was rapidly losing patience with the morning's entertainment.

"Mrs. Henderson!" Donald called out cheerfully. "Franklin's just admiring your beautiful garden. He's got very sophisticated taste, you can tell he recognizes quality landscaping when he sees it."

"Get that pig out of my roses!"

"Absolutely. Right away. Franklin!" Donald tried to grab the pig, but Franklin apparently considered this an interesting new game. He dodged away from Donald's reaching hands and trotted toward the far corner of the Henderson garden, where he discovered a small vegetable patch.

"DONALD TRUMP!"

The voice came from the direction of the Trump house and belonged unmistakably to his mother. Donald looked over the fence to see his parents' car in the driveway, two hours earlier than expected, and his mother standing in the kitchen doorway surveying what Franklin had left of her previously organized home.

"Franklin," Donald said quietly. "I think we might need to discuss our partnership terms."

Franklin looked up from Mrs. Henderson's lettuce and made a soft honking sound that Donald chose to interpret as understanding. Then, with perfect timing, he trotted back toward the fence that separated the two properties.

The problem was that while Franklin could squeeze under the fence in one direction, going back proved more challenging. He was slightly larger now, having spent the morning sampling various neighbourhood delicacies, and the fence opening that had seemed perfectly adequate earlier was now distinctly tight.

Franklin got his head and front legs through the gap, but his midsection stuck firmly. His back legs scrambled for purchase in the Henderson garden while his front half waggled frantically in the Trump backyard. He honked with increasing volume and decreasing dignity.

"DONALD!" his mother called again.

"I'll be right there!" Donald called back, then turned to the stuck pig. "Franklin, work with me here. We're both in trouble if we can't figure this out."

Eddie appeared on the other side of the fence. "Push from your side, I'll pull from this side."

"Wait," Donald said. "If we pull too hard, we might hurt him."

"If we don't get him unstuck, your parents are going to hurt both of you," Eddie pointed out.

They spent the next five minutes engaged in a delicate pig extraction operation, with Donald pushing carefully from behind while Eddie pulled on Franklin's front legs. Franklin contributed by honking continuously and occasionally trying to bite anyone within reach.

Finally, with a sound like a cork coming out of a bottle, Franklin popped through the fence and landed in an undignified heap in his own backyard. He stood up, shook himself off, and looked around as if nothing particularly interesting had happened.

"DONALD TRUMP, GET IN THIS HOUSE RIGHT NOW!"

Donald looked at the chaos of the garage sale, where Frankie was still trying to handle customers who wanted to buy things. He looked at Franklin, who was now investigating the remains of the tomato garden with renewed interest. He looked at his torn, dirty suit and his grass-stained hands and his complete lack of a plan for what to do next.

Then he took a deep breath, straightened his father's tie, and walked toward the house with as much dignity as he could manage.

"Coming, Mom!"

Behind him, Franklin discovered the sprinkler system and accidentally turned it on by stepping on the control mechanism. Water began spraying in all directions, soaking the remaining garage sale merchandise and causing the last few customers to run for cover.

Eddie, standing in the sudden downpour, looked at Frankie. "Think this is going to be a long summer?"

Frankie, clutching the soggy cash box, grinned. "Are you kidding? This is the best garage sale I've ever seen."

Franklin, now happily rolling in the mud that had been Mrs. Trump's prize-winning roses, honked in agreement.

From inside the house came the sound of Donald's voice, rising and falling in what was clearly a very animated explanation. Occasionally, the voice of Mrs. Trump could be heard asking pointed questions about golf clubs and broken dishes and the presence of livestock in her kitchen.

But even through the kitchen window, Donald's voice carried a note of enthusiasm that suggested he was already working on his next big idea.

After all, the summer was just getting started, and he now had a business partner with genuine star quality. Together, they were going to build something tremendous. The best you've ever seen.

Franklin honked once more and settled down for a nap in the muddy garden, apparently satisfied with his first day as a business partner.

The garage sale was officially over, but Donald Trump's summer of entrepreneurial adventure was just beginning.

The Lemonade Corporate Ladder

Three days after what Donald had taken to calling "The Great Garage Sale Success Story" (and what his parents called "The Day Franklin Destroyed Everything"), Donald found himself in a considerably less favourable negotiating position.

He was grounded until further notice. His allowance had been suspended indefinitely to pay for the replacement of his mother's good China. The golf club's situation had resulted in what his father called "a serious conversation about property rights and business ethics", which was really just a long lecture about not selling other people's things without permission. And Franklin Delano Roosevelt was now living in a hastily constructed pen in the far corner of the backyard, where he spent his days planning what Donald was convinced were his next entrepreneurial ventures.

But Donald Trump didn't stay down for long. By Thursday morning, he'd identified a new opportunity that would solve all his current problems while demonstrating the kind of innovative thinking that separated leaders from followers.

He was going to revolutionize the lemonade business.

"The problem with traditional lemonade stands," Donald explained to Eddie and Frankie as they sat in the shade of the maple tree in Donald's backyard, "is that they're thinking too small. One kid, one table, one flavour, that's amateur hour. We're going to create a lemonade enterprise that actually understands customer service and market differentiation."

Eddie, who'd been sceptical of Donald's business ventures even before the pig incident, looked unconvinced. "Donald, it's lemonade. You squeeze lemons, add water and sugar, and sell it for a dime. What's to revolutionize?"

"Everything!" Donald stood up and began pacing, his enthusiasm building as he spoke. "See, that's exactly the kind of limited thinking that keeps the lemonade industry stuck in the past. We're going to offer multiple flavour options, professional presentation, and premium customer service. Nobody does lemonade like we're going to do lemonade."

From his pen in the corner of the yard, Franklin honked what Donald chose to interpret as encouragement.

"Plus," Donald continued, "we've got Franklin as our promotional asset. People already know him from the garage sale. He's got name recognition in this neighbourhood now. That's marketing gold."

Frankie, whose faith in Donald's schemes remained unshaken despite recent evidence, leaned forward with interest. "So, what's the plan?"

Donald pulled out a notebook where he'd been sketching business diagrams late into the previous night. "Multi-station operation. We set up three tables along the sidewalk in front of the house. Station, One handles classic lemonade, that's our baseline product for traditional customers. Station Two offers premium flavours, pink lemonade, strawberry lemonade, maybe even limeade for the sophisticated market. Station Three is our innovation lab, custom mixes, special requests, whatever the customer wants."

"Who's going to run three stations?" Eddie asked.

"Division of responsibility," Donald said, consulting his notebook. "Frankie, you're head of Traditional Operations. Eddie, you're

Director of Premium Flavors. I'm Chief Executive Officer and Customer Relations Manager. Franklin will be our mascot and quality control specialist."

Eddie looked at Franklin, who was currently trying to scratch his back against the fence post. "Quality control?"

"Franklin's got natural taste. He knows good food when he sees it. If Franklin approves of our product, customers will trust the quality guarantee."

"Donald," Eddie said slowly, "Franklin ate half your mom's garden and then broke into the house and demolished the kitchen. I'm not sure he's the best spokesperson for quality control."

"That shows initiative and thorough investigation skills," Donald replied. "Franklin doesn't settle for surface-level evaluation. He really digs deep into the customer experience."

The boys spent the rest of Thursday morning planning their lemonade enterprise. Donald drew up organizational charts, pricing strategies, and what he called "operational protocols." They would launch on Friday morning, targeting the weekend foot traffic and establishing market dominance before any competing operations could respond.

"The key," Donald explained as they worked on calculating startup costs, "is professional presentation. We can't look like some amateur neighbourhood kids trying to make pocket money. We need to look like a legitimate business that just happens to be run by young entrepreneurs."

This meant investing in proper signage, uniforms (matching t-shirts that Donald planned to borrow from his father's collection), and what Donald called "infrastructure improvements", which mostly involved constructing a more elaborate table setup and creating an actual business system for handling orders and payments.

"How much money do we need to get started?" Frankie asked.

Donald consulted his notebook, where he'd written calculations in the margins and drawn arrows connecting various costs and projected revenues. "Initial investment should be around five dollars for lemons, sugar, and supplies. But I'm projecting first-day revenues of at least fifteen dollars, possibly twenty if we get good foot traffic."

"Where are we getting the five dollars?" Eddie asked.

This was, Donald realized, an excellent question. His allowance was suspended, his garage sale profits had been confiscated to pay for household damages, and his parents had made it clear that additional funding for entrepreneurial ventures was not currently available.

"Creative financing," Donald said. "I've been thinking about this, and I believe I can secure a short-term loan from my mother for startup costs. She'll get her investment back plus interest within forty-eight hours."

Eddie and Frankie exchanged looks. Donald's relationship with his parents had been somewhat strained since the pig incident, and the likelihood of Mrs. Trump investing in another of Donald's business ventures seemed questionable at best.

But Donald had been thinking about this challenge, and he'd developed what he considered a foolproof approach.

That evening, Donald approached his mother while she was reading in the living room. He'd changed out of his father's suit and was wearing his most responsible-looking clothes, clean jeans and a button-down shirt that actually fit him properly.

"Mom," he said, settling into the chair across from her with the serious expression he used for important conversations. "I wanted to talk to you about making amends for what happened with Franklin on Tuesday."

Mrs. Trump looked up from her magazine. Since the pig incident, she'd been viewing Donald's overtures with considerable suspicion. "What kind of amends?"

"Well, I've been thinking that the best way to show how sorry I am would be to earn back the money for the dishes and the garden damage through honest work rather than just having it taken out of my allowance."

This was, Donald felt, a strong opening position. It demonstrated both remorse and work ethic, two qualities his parents valued highly.

"Go on," Mrs. Trump said.

"So, I've developed a plan for a small business venture that would allow me to earn back what I owe while also learning valuable lessons about responsibility and financial management."

Donald had practiced this pitch in front of his bedroom mirror for twenty minutes. He was hitting all the right notes, responsibility, learning, financial awareness.

"What kind of business venture?" Mrs. Trump asked, though her tone suggested she was already anticipating complications.

"A lemonade stand. But not just any lemonade stand, a properly organized, customer-focused operation that would serve the neighbourhood and provide a genuine service while teaching me important lessons about entrepreneurship and customer relations."

Mrs. Trump set down her magazine. "Donald, how much money are you asking for?"

"Just five dollars for startup costs. Lemons, sugar, cups, basic supplies. I'll pay you back the five dollars plus fifty cents interest by Sunday evening. That's ten percent return on investment in less than a week. You can't get those kinds of returns from the bank."

Donald was particularly proud of the interest calculation, which he'd learned about from his father's business magazines. Offering interest showed that he understood the time value of money and was serious about treating this as a legitimate business transaction rather than just asking for money.

Mrs. Trump was quiet for a long moment, studying her son's face. Donald kept his expression serious and responsible, the way he imagined successful businessmen looked when they were proposing important deals.

"Five dollars," she said finally.

"Five dollars," Donald confirmed.

"And you'll pay back five-fifty by Sunday."

"Guaranteed."

"And Franklin stays in his pen during business hours."

Donald hadn't actually planned on keeping Franklin contained during the lemonade operation, but this seemed like a reasonable compromise. "Franklin will maintain appropriate professional boundaries."

Mrs. Trump reached for her purse. "Donald, I'm going to give you this money because I think learning to run a business could be good for you. But if this turns into anything like Tuesday's situation, there won't be any more business ventures this summer. Are we clear?"

"Perfectly clear," Donald said, accepting the five-dollar bill with the solemnity the moment deserved. "This is going to be the most professional lemonade operation you've ever seen."

Friday morning dawned clear and warm, perfect lemonade weather. Donald had spent the previous evening preparing what he called "operational materials", hand-lettered signs advertising "TRUMP'S PREMIUM LEMONADE - FRESH DAILY - SATISFACTION GUARANTEED," paper cups arranged in neat stacks, and a cash box improvised from an old cigar box his father had given him.

He'd also convinced his mother to let him use her good tablecloth again, promising that this time there would be no livestock involved in the customer service process.

"Remember," Donald told Eddie and Frankie as they set up the three-table operation along the sidewalk in front of the house, "we're not just selling lemonade. We're selling an experience. Professional service, quality ingredients, and attention to detail that you can't get from the competition."

"What competition?" Eddie asked. "Nobody else on this block is running a lemonade stand."

"Exactly," Donald said. "We're establishing market dominance before anyone else even realizes the opportunity exists. By the time copycats try to enter the market, we'll already have customer loyalty and brand recognition."

The setup looked impressive, Donald had to admit. Three tables covered with his mother's tablecloth, each with its own clearly marked signs and properly arranged supplies. Station One featured classic lemonade in a large glass pitcher with floating lemon slices for visual appeal. Station Two offered pink lemonade and what Donald called "strawberry fusion," which was really just regular lemonade with a few drops of food colouring and some mashed strawberries floating in it. Station Three was designated for "custom creations" and featured an array of flavour additives that Donald had assembled from the kitchen spice cabinet.

"This looks pretty good," Frankie admitted, stepping back to admire their work.

"It looks professional," Donald agreed. "Now remember, we're not just taking orders, we're consulting with customers about their beverage needs and providing personalized recommendations. Customer service is what separates premium operations from street-corner amateurs."

From his pen in the backyard, Franklin honked as if he wanted to contribute to the morning briefing.

"Franklin approves," Donald announced. "That's our quality seal right there."

Their first customer was Mr. Chen from two blocks over, who was out for his morning walk and stopped to examine their setup with the interest of someone who appreciated attention to detail.

"Good morning, sir!" Donald called out, immediately assuming his professional posture. "Welcome to Trump's Premium Lemonade. We offer the finest freshly made lemonade in the neighbourhood, with multiple flavour options and customized service. What can we create for you today?"

Mr. Chen smiled at Donald's enthusiasm. "Just regular lemonade, please."

"Excellent choice," Donald said, guiding him toward Station One. "Frankie, one classic lemonade for Mr. Chen. Our classic recipe uses fresh lemons, pure cane sugar, and filtered water in proportions that have been carefully calibrated for optimal taste and refreshment."

Frankie poured the lemonade with obvious care, adding exactly two ice cubes and a paper straw cut to the perfect length. "That'll be ten cents, sir."

Mr. Chen handed over a dime and took a sip. "That's very good lemonade."

"We guarantee satisfaction," Donald said, making a note in his order log. "If you're not completely happy with your purchase, we'll provide a full refund or create a custom replacement at no additional charge."

Mr. Chen walked away looking genuinely pleased, and Donald felt the familiar surge of confidence that came with successful customer interaction. This was going to work. This was going to be tremendous.

Their next customers were the Kowalski twins, who approached the operation with the serious expressions of people conducting important business.

"We want to try the pink kind," announced the first twin.

"An excellent selection," Donald said, directing them toward Station Two. "Eddie, two premium pink lemonades for our valued customers. The pink lemonade uses the same high-quality base as our classic variety, but with the addition of natural fruit essences that create both visual appeal and enhanced flavour complexity."

Eddie poured the pink lemonade, which looked significantly more appealing than it had in the pitcher thanks to the morning sunlight and properly arranged presentation. The twins each handed over their dimes and took appreciative sips.

"It tastes like regular lemonade," said the second twin.

"But pink," added the first.

"Exactly!" Donald said. "You're experiencing the perfect balance of familiar quality with innovative presentation. That's what we call 'elevated classic', taking something everyone loves and making it even better through careful attention to detail."

The twins seemed satisfied with this explanation and walked away comparing the relative pinkness of their drinks.

By ten-thirty, Donald had served twelve customers and made one dollar and twenty cents. More importantly, word was spreading about the new lemonade operation. He could see people pointing toward their setup as they walked by, and several customers had mentioned that they'd heard about the lemonade stand from neighbours.

"This is working," Donald told Eddie and Frankie during a brief operational break. "We're building customer base and brand awareness exactly like I projected. By next week, we could be expanding to additional locations."

"Additional locations?" Eddie asked.

"Strategic market expansion," Donald explained. "Once we've saturated this immediate area, we identify high-traffic zones throughout the neighbourhood and establish satellite operations. Scale up gradually while maintaining quality control."

That's when Franklin decided to contribute to the morning's success.

Despite Donald's promise to keep the pig contained during business hours, Franklin had apparently been observing the lemonade operation with great interest. He'd been unusually quiet in his pen, which Donald had interpreted as cooperation. What Franklin had actually been doing was working on the latch mechanism with the same systematic approach he'd applied to his crate on Tuesday.

The first sign of trouble was when Mrs. Rodriguez, who'd been approaching Station Three to inquire about custom flavour options, suddenly stopped and pointed toward the backyard.

"Is that pig supposed to be loose?"

Donald turned to see Franklin trotting purposefully across the lawn toward their operation, having somehow escaped from his pen. He was moving with the focused determination of someone who had a specific goal in mind.

"Franklin!" Donald called out. "You're supposed to be in your designated area!"

But Franklin had spotted the setup and was clearly interested in participating. He approached Station Two, where Eddie was preparing another pink lemonade, and began investigating the ingredients with professional curiosity.

"Uh, Donald?" Eddie said nervously. "What should I do?"

"Just keep working," Donald replied, trying to maintain calm in front of their customer. "Franklin's conducting a quality inspection. He takes our standards very seriously."

Franklin stuck his snout into the pitcher of pink lemonade and took a long, appreciative drink. Then he looked up at Eddie and made a soft honking sound that could reasonably be interpreted as approval.

Mrs. Rodriguez laughed. "Well, if the pig likes it, it must be good."

This gave Donald an idea that was either brilliant or disastrous, and in his current state of entrepreneurial enthusiasm, he couldn't tell the difference.

"Ladies and gentlemen!" he called out to the small crowd that had gathered to watch Franklin's taste test. "You're witnessing our exclusive quality assurance process! Franklin here is our official beverage consultant, he only approves products that meet our premium standards!"

Franklin, apparently understanding that he was being discussed, performed a small bow that sent the crowd into delighted laughter.

"So, if Franklin approves of a flavour," Donald continued, warming to the concept, "you know you're getting something special. Franklin's Guarantee, if it's good enough for our pig, it's perfect for you."

This was completely improvised, but the crowd seemed to love it. Several people immediately requested lemonades that had received "Franklin's approval," and Donald found himself taking orders faster than his team could fill them.

The problem was that Franklin interpreted his new role as quality consultant very literally. He moved from station to station, sampling each variety of lemonade and occasionally making suggestions (communicated through honks and snorts) for improvements. When he particularly enjoyed something, he would sit and offer his hoof to customers, which everyone found charming.

But Franklin's standards were high, and he wasn't shy about expressing disapproval. When Eddie accidentally made a batch of pink lemonade that was too sweet, Franklin took one taste and immediately turned his back on the entire pitcher, communicating his rejection so clearly that the watching customers broke into applause.

"Even our pig has standards," Donald announced, turning Franklin's critique into a selling point. "That's the kind of quality control you get with a premium operation."

Eddie had to dump the rejected batch and start over, but the customers seemed genuinely impressed by the thoroughness of the quality assurance process.

By noon, the lemonade stand was generating more attention than Donald had imagined possible. They had a steady stream of customers, several people taking pictures of Franklin in his role as beverage consultant, and what Donald recognized as genuine word-of-mouth marketing happening in real time.

They'd also made three dollars and forty cents, which was approaching what Donald considered serious money.

That's when the Feinberg twins arrived.

Madeline and Josephine Feinberg were twelve-year-old identical twins who lived four blocks away and had a reputation for efficiency that bordered on the supernatural. They could organize a neighbourhood scavenger hunt, coordinate a block party, or run a bake sale with the precision of military operations. They were also, Donald had to admit, considerably better at follow-through than he was.

They approached the lemonade operation with the focused attention of competitors conducting market research.

"Interesting setup," Madeline said, surveying the three-station arrangement.

"Quality standards," Josephine added, watching Franklin investigate a fresh pitcher of strawberry fusion.

Donald felt his confidence waver slightly. The Feinberg twins had a way of making even his best ideas seem somehow amateur by comparison. But he was committed to maintaining professional confidence in front of customers.

"Madeline! Josephine!" he called out with forced enthusiasm. "Welcome to Trump's Premium Lemonade! What can we create for you today?"

"We're just observing," Madeline replied. "Market research."

"Understanding the competition," Josephine added.

Donald's smile became slightly more strained. "Competition? I wasn't aware there was any competition in the local lemonade sector."

"There will be," the twins said in perfect unison.

They spent the next ten minutes examining every aspect of the operation, the pricing, the presentation, the flavour options, and especially Franklin's role in the quality assurance process. They took notes in matching notebooks and occasionally whispered to each other in what sounded like some kind of tactical planning language.

Finally, they approached Donald at his position behind Station Three.

"Nice pig," Madeline said.

"Excellent marketing concept," Josephine added.

"Thank you," Donald replied cautiously. "Franklin's a key part of our customer experience strategy."

"We'll be launching our operation on Monday," Madeline informed him.

"Advanced customer service," Josephine continued. "Professional ingredients."

"Home delivery," they concluded together.

Then they walked away, leaving Donald with the distinct feeling that he'd just been professionally assessed and found wanting.

"Home delivery?" Frankie whispered. "Can they do that?"

"Anyone can deliver lemonade," Donald said, though his voice lacked its usual confidence. "The question is whether they can deliver the kind of quality and customer experience that builds real brand loyalty."

But for the rest of the afternoon, Donald found himself distracted by thoughts of the Feinberg twins and their promised Monday launch. Home delivery was, he had to admit, a significant competitive advantage. It solved the location problem, expanded the potential customer base, and offered convenience that a fixed operation couldn't match.

"We need to accelerate our expansion timeline," Donald announced during the afternoon break, when they'd temporarily closed for what he called "strategic planning and inventory replenishment."

"Accelerate how?" Eddie asked.

"Multiple locations, premium service options, and extended hours. If they're going to compete on convenience, we'll compete on scale and quality."

Donald's expansion plans involved setting up additional lemonade stations at strategic locations throughout the neighbourhood, the corner near the bus stop, the park entrance, maybe even a mobile operation that could respond to demand in real time.

"Donald," Eddie said carefully, "we barely have enough people to run this one location. How are we going to manage multiple stations?"

"Delegation and strategic partnerships," Donald replied. "We recruit additional team members and train them in our operational standards. Build a network of Trump-approved lemonade professionals."

This sounded impressive in theory, but Eddie could see several practical problems. "Who's going to train them? And who's going to supervise all these locations?"

"Management structure," Donald said, consulting his notebook. "I'll be Regional Director of Operations, overseeing quality and strategy. You and Frankie become Station Managers, responsible for training and supervision at your assigned locations. Franklin continues as Chief Quality Officer, rotating between locations to maintain standards."

The afternoon brought new challenges that tested Donald's expansion theories. A group of younger kids from the elementary school had heard about the lemonade stand and arrived expecting to be entertained by Franklin's quality control performance. Franklin, however, had apparently decided that he'd done enough beverage consulting for one day and was more interested in napping in the shade under Station Two.

"Where's the pig?" demanded a six-year-old named Tommy, who'd clearly been promised pig-related entertainment.

"Franklin's taking a strategic break," Donald explained. "Quality consultants need to rest their palates between tastings to maintain accuracy."

"But I want to see him test the lemonade!"

Donald looked at Franklin, who was definitely asleep and showed no interest in participating in customer entertainment. "Franklin operates on his own schedule. That's part of what makes his recommendations so valuable, he only performs when he's genuinely motivated."

This was a diplomatic way of saying that Donald had no control over when Franklin chose to engage with the business, but the customers seemed to accept it.

The real problem came when Franklin woke up and decided that he was thirsty.

Instead of politely requesting a sample from one of the designated testing pitchers, Franklin walked directly to Station One and began drinking from the main serving pitcher, the one that Frankie had been using to serve customers all afternoon.

"Franklin!" Donald called out in alarm. "That's customer inventory!"

But Franklin was clearly enjoying the classic lemonade and wasn't interested in interrupting his refreshment break. He drank steadily while a line of customers watched with amusement and growing concern about sanitary practices.

"Is that sanitary?" asked Mrs. Patterson, who'd been waiting to order two cups of strawberry fusion.

Donald's mind raced through possible responses. "Franklin maintains very high personal hygiene standards," he said finally. "And he's our quality control specialist, so he's naturally very careful about contamination issues."

This explanation satisfied exactly no one.

"But he's a pig," pointed out Tommy the six-year-old. "Pigs are dirty."

"That's a common misconception," Donald replied, though he was beginning to panic about the sanitary implications of Franklin's direct-pitcher approach. "Pigs are actually very clean animals when they're properly cared for. Much cleaner than most people realize."

Franklin, having finished his evaluation of the classic lemonade, moved on to Station Two and began sampling the pink lemonade with the same thorough approach.

"Okay," said Mrs. Patterson, "I think I'll come back later."

She left, along with three other customers who'd been waiting in line. Donald watched his afternoon revenues walking away and realized that Franklin's quality control methods, while entertaining, might need some refinement.

"New operational protocol," Donald announced. "Franklin gets his own designated testing samples. Customer inventory stays separate from quality control processes."

This should have solved the problem, but Franklin had apparently decided that his role as quality consultant entitled him to unlimited sampling privileges. When Frankie tried to redirect him toward a small cup of lemonade specifically set aside for testing purposes, Franklin ignored it and headed straight for the large pitcher of strawberry fusion.

"Franklin, you're compromising our sanitation standards," Donald said, attempting to guide the pig away from customer inventory.

Franklin looked at Donald with what could only be described as disdain and continued drinking from the pitcher.

The situation deteriorated rapidly from there. Franklin's expanded role in quality control began interfering with actual customer service. He would approve of some flavours enthusiastically (causing minor stampedes as customers rushed to order "Franklin-approved" drinks) and reject others completely (leaving Donald with unsellable inventory that had been officially condemned by their quality consultant).

Even worse, Franklin had developed opinions about customer service itself. When Eddie accidentally shortchanged Mr. Kowalski by a nickel, Franklin noticed and began honking until the error was corrected. When Frankie forgot to add the regulation two ice cubes to a pink lemonade order, Franklin positioned himself between the customer and the drink until the proper ice was added.

"Your pig is very strict about procedures," observed Mrs. Chen, who'd watched Franklin reject three consecutive batches of custom-mixed lemonade because they didn't meet his apparently sophisticated standards.

"Franklin takes our quality commitments seriously," Donald replied, though he was beginning to wonder if hiring a pig as quality control had been the strategic advantage he'd intended.

By three o'clock, Donald's carefully planned lemonade enterprise was generating attention throughout the neighbourhood, but not necessarily the kind of attention he wanted. People were coming by specifically to watch Franklin's quality control performances, but many of them left without actually purchasing anything.

Franklin had become the star of the operation, but his standards were so high and his methods so disruptive that actual lemonade sales were suffering.

"We need to adjust our operational structure," Donald told Eddie and Frankie during an emergency strategy session while Franklin napped under the table. "Franklin's quality control is too effective. He's rejecting inventory that's probably perfectly acceptable to normal customers."

"Maybe we could limit his testing to once per hour?" Frankie suggested.

"Or maybe we could just serve the lemonade without having a pig stick his nose in it?" Eddie added.

Donald considered these options, but both felt like steps backward rather than forward. Franklin was clearly a customer draw, people loved him, and his presence made their operation unique in the neighbourhood. The problem was managing his involvement without letting it interfere with actual business.

"What we need," Donald said slowly, "is to leverage Franklin's appeal while maintaining operational efficiency. Keep the entertainment value but streamline the quality control process."

That's when Franklin solved the problem himself.

A customer approached Station One requesting classic lemonade. Frankie began to pour from the main pitcher, but before he could complete the order, Franklin woke up and trotted over to investigate. Instead of drinking from the customer pitcher, however, Franklin sat down next to the table and extended his hoof toward the customer in his signature greeting.

The customer, delighted by Franklin's attention, shook the offered hoof and immediately handed over not just the standard ten cents, but fifteen cents. "Keep the change," she said. "That pig is adorable."

Donald stared at the extra nickel and felt the kind of revelation that successful entrepreneurs probably experienced all the time. Franklin didn't need to taste-test every batch of lemonade to be valuable to the operation. His simple presence and customer interaction were worth more than any quality control function.

"New strategy," Donald announced. "Franklin is now Director of Customer Relations. His job is to greet customers and make them feel welcome, not to evaluate beverage quality."

This worked brilliantly for approximately twenty minutes.

Franklin embraced his new role with enthusiasm, greeting each customer with his signature hoof-shake and occasionally performing his sitting trick when he sensed that extra entertainment was warranted. Tips increased, customer satisfaction clearly improved, and Donald's confidence returned to its normal high levels.

The problem was that Franklin still had opinions about quality, and he wasn't shy about expressing them.

When Eddie accidentally served a customer a cup of lemonade that had been sitting in the sun too long and had become unpleasantly warm, Franklin noticed. Instead of honking his disapproval, however, he simply walked over to the customer and gently knocked the cup out of her hand with his snout.

"Franklin!" Donald called out in alarm as lemonade splashed across the sidewalk.

But the customer was laughing. "I think your pig just saved me from a bad drink," she said. "That lemonade was pretty warm."

Eddie quickly poured a fresh, properly chilled replacement, and the customer left fifteen cents instead of the standard ten.

"Franklin's got quality standards even when he's not officially quality testing," Frankie observed.

Donald watched Franklin return to his greeting position and realized that his pig was turning out to be a better businessman than he was. Franklin understood customer service instinctively, he had natural timing for both entertainment and quality intervention, and he was generating tips that significantly improved their profit margins.

"Franklin," Donald said quietly, "you might be the best business partner I've ever had."

Franklin honked once and returned his attention to the next approaching customer.

The afternoon's success was interrupted by the sound of a bicycle bell and the arrival of Lisa Chen, Mr. Chen's daughter and the girl Donald had been trying to work up the courage to talk to all summer. She pedalled up to the lemonade operation on her blue Schwinn, her dark hair tied back with a yellow ribbon that matched her sundress.

Donald immediately felt his professional confidence desert him and be replaced by the tongue-tied nervousness that seemed to affect him whenever Lisa was around.

"Hi, Donald," Lisa said, parking her bike and approaching Station Three with a smile. "My dad said you're running a really professional operation here."

"Oh," Donald managed. "Yeah. Professional. Very professional. We've got... quality control and... Franklin."

Lisa looked at Franklin, who was sitting politely next to the table like a trained customer service representative. "He's really cute. Can I shake his hand?"

Franklin, demonstrating the social skills that Donald envied, immediately offered his hoof and performed his sitting trick without being asked.

"He's amazing," Lisa said, scratching behind Franklin's ears. "How did you train him to do that?"

"Natural talent," Donald replied, his voice cracking slightly. "Franklin's got instinctive customer relations abilities. He understands people."

"And what about you?" Lisa asked, looking directly at Donald with the kind of attention that made his brain stop working properly. "What's your role in this operation?"

"I'm the... I'm Chief Executive Officer and Director of Strategic Planning," Donald said, trying to sound impressive while not looking directly at Lisa's smile.

"That sounds important," Lisa said. "What kind of strategic planning?"

Donald's mind went completely blank. All his carefully prepared business vocabulary disappeared, leaving him standing there in his father's oversized suit jacket (which he'd worn again for professional credibility) making what he was sure were unintelligent facial expressions.

"Well," he said finally, "we're planning... strategies. For the lemonade. Business strategies."

Franklin, apparently sensing that Donald needed assistance, stood up and gently nudged him toward Lisa. Then, with perfect timing, Franklin knocked over the small tip jar that Donald had positioned next to Station Three, sending coins rolling across the sidewalk.

"Oh no!" Lisa said, immediately kneeling to help collect the scattered money.

Donald knelt down beside her, grateful for an activity that didn't require coherent conversation. As they gathered nickels and dimes, their hands occasionally brushed, which made Donald's heart do things that were probably visible from space.

"Thanks," he said when they'd retrieved all the coins. "Franklin's still learning about proper cash handling procedures."

Lisa laughed. "He's probably better at customer service than most adults. I've never seen a pig shake hands before."

"Franklin's special," Donald said, feeling slightly more confident now that they were talking about his pig rather than his business qualifications. "He's got personality."

"He definitely does." Lisa stood up and dusted off her dress. "So, what kind of lemonade would you recommend for someone who's never tried your premium varieties?"

This was business territory, where Donald felt more comfortable. "Well, that depends on your flavour preferences and refreshment needs. Are you looking for classic familiarity or innovative taste experiences?"

"Surprise me," Lisa said.

Donald felt a surge of panic. This was clearly some kind of test, and choosing the wrong lemonade recommendation could be catastrophic for his chances of ever having a normal conversation with Lisa Chen.

"Eddie," he called out, "one custom creation for our valued customer. Something that demonstrates our full range of capabilities."

Eddie looked at the array of flavour additives and began mixing what Donald hoped would be an impressive combination of strawberry essence, extra lemon, and a careful sprinkle of what the spice cabinet had labelled as "fruit flavour enhancer."

Franklin watched the mixing process with professional interest and, when Eddie finished, approached the cup for his official evaluation.

Franklin sniffed the custom creation, took a small taste, and then sat down and offered his hoof to Lisa, the official Franklin seal of approval.

"Franklin guarantees it," Donald said, praying that Eddie had created something actually drinkable.

Lisa accepted the cup, took a sip, and smiled. "That's really good. What's in it?"

"Trade secret," Donald replied. "But I can tell you that it represents our most advanced flavour technology."

Lisa finished the entire cup and handed over fifteen cents without being asked. "Keep the change. That pig is worth the extra tip."

As she rode away on her bicycle, Donald felt like he'd just won some kind of important victory. Franklin had approved of his choice, Lisa had enjoyed the product, and he'd managed to complete an entire customer interaction without saying anything completely embarrassing.

"She likes you," Frankie said quietly.

"She likes the lemonade," Donald corrected. "And Franklin. This was a successful customer service interaction, nothing more."

But he was smiling as he said it, and Eddie noticed that Donald carefully wrote "custom creation - 15¢ + 5¢ tip" in his notebook with more attention than he'd given to any other transaction of the day.

The afternoon continued successfully until Franklin decided to expand his customer relations role to include neighbourhood outreach.

It started when Franklin noticed a dog walker passing by on the opposite side of the street. Franklin had been sitting politely next to Station Two, fulfilling his greeting duties, when he spotted the golden retriever and apparently decided that customer service should extend to all neighbourhood residents, regardless of species.

Franklin trotted across the street with the confidence of someone who understood traffic patterns, approached the golden retriever, and offered his hoof for a formal introduction.

The dog, surprised but friendly, sniffed Franklin's hoof and wagged his tail. Franklin honked politely. The dog barked once in response. Franklin sat down and performed his trick sitting position.

The dog owner, an elderly man Donald didn't recognize, was delighted by Franklin's diplomatic approach to interspecies relations.

"Well, I'll be damned," the man said, watching Franklin and the golden retriever conduct what appeared to be a formal negotiation about territory and sniffing privileges. "That's the politest pig I've ever seen."

Donald seized the opportunity. "That's Franklin Roosevelt, our Director of Customer Relations!" he called across the street. "He's part of our premium lemonade service! Would you like to try our neighbourhood-famous quality?"

The man looked intrigued and crossed the street with his dog, who seemed eager to continue the conversation with Franklin. "Neighbourhood-famous, eh?"

"Franklin's personally approved every recipe," Donald said, falling into his sales routine. "We guarantee satisfaction or your money back."

The man bought a classic lemonade and let his dog sniff Franklin while both animals seemed to discuss whatever it is that dogs and pigs find mutually interesting. He left a nickel tip and promised to tell his neighbours about "the lemonade stand with the professional pig."

Donald was feeling triumphant about this expansion of their customer base when he noticed that Franklin and the golden retriever had attracted additional attention. Two more dog walkers had stopped to see what was happening, and a small crowd of children had gathered to watch the inter-animal diplomacy.

"Franklin's conducting community outreach," Donald announced to Eddie and Frankie. "This is exactly the kind of grassroots marketing that builds sustainable customer relationships."

But Franklin's community outreach was becoming more ambitious by the minute. Having successfully established diplomatic relations with the golden retriever, he apparently decided to introduce himself to every dog, cat, and small child in the immediate vicinity.

This meant that Franklin was no longer stationed at the lemonade operation but was instead conducting a roving meet-and-greet throughout the neighbourhood. Donald could see him across the street, shaking hands with a toddler while the toddler's mother laughed and took pictures. Then Franklin spotted a cat sitting on a porch and trotted over to attempt formal introductions.

"Should we go get him?" Frankie asked.

"Franklin knows what he's doing," Donald said, though he was beginning to wonder if Franklin's customer relations initiatives were becoming counterproductive to actual lemonade sales. "He's building brand awareness throughout the target demographic."

The cat, it turned out, was less receptive to Franklin's diplomatic overtures than the dog had been. Instead of engaging in polite interspecies negotiation, the cat took one look at Franklin's approaching snout and launched itself onto the nearest tree, where it clung to the bark and made sounds that could generously be called unfriendly.

Franklin, apparently interpreting this as playful engagement, positioned himself at the base of the tree and began honking encouragement for the cat to come down and participate in proper introductions.

"Franklin!" Donald called from across the street. "We need you back at headquarters!"

But Franklin was committed to his community outreach mission. He honked several more times at the treed cat, performed his sitting trick for the growing crowd of spectators, and then trotted off toward the next block to continue his neighbourhood tour.

Donald realized that he had a choice to make. He could abandon the lemonade operation to chase Franklin around the neighbourhood, or he could trust that Franklin would eventually return and focus on serving the customers who were actually standing in front of the tables waiting to purchase beverages.

"Eddie, take over customer relations," Donald said. "I'm going to conduct mobile management supervision."

Donald spent the next twenty minutes tracking Franklin through the neighbourhood while trying to maintain the professional appearance of someone whose business partner hadn't gone completely rogue. He found Franklin three blocks away, holding court in the playground where he'd apparently discovered that children were extremely generous with attention and snacks.

"Franklin," Donald said, approaching the crowd of kids who were taking turns feeding Franklin pieces of their sandwiches. "We need to discuss operational priorities."

Franklin looked up from a peanut butter and jelly sandwich and honked what Donald chose to interpret as acknowledgment.

"Listen," Donald said quietly, sitting down next to Franklin while the children continued their impromptu feeding session. "I appreciate your initiative with community outreach. But we've got a business to run, and our customers expect to see you at the lemonade station."

Franklin considered this and then stood up, apparently ready to return to work. But instead of heading back toward the house, he trotted over to the playground water fountain and began drinking deeply.

It took Donald several minutes to realize what Franklin was actually doing. The pig hadn't abandoned his quality control responsibilities, he was hydrating properly so he could continue his beverage consulting work. Franklin was taking his job seriously enough to maintain his palate with fresh water between tastings.

"You're actually thinking about this scientifically," Donald said, impressed despite himself. "That's the kind of professional approach that makes the difference between amateur operations and premium services."

Franklin finished drinking and looked at Donald expectantly.

"All right," Donald said. "Let's go back to work."

The walk back to the lemonade stand gave Donald time to think about the morning's lessons. Franklin was definitely an asset to the operation, but managing his contributions required more strategic thinking than Donald had initially planned. The pig had his own ideas about customer service, quality control, and community relations, and those ideas didn't always align with traditional business practices.

But the customers loved Franklin, and Franklin's involvement was generating both sales and word-of-mouth marketing that no conventional lemonade stand could match. The trick was going to be finding ways to channel Franklin's natural abilities while maintaining operational control.

When they returned to the house, Donald discovered that Eddie and Frankie had sold six more cups of lemonade in his absence, including two custom creations that customers had specifically requested because they wanted to try "whatever Franklin would approve of."

"People keep asking when Franklin's coming back," Eddie reported. "I think we've got customers who are coming by just to see him."

Donald looked at Franklin, who had resumed his position next to Station Two and was greeting returning customers with his professional hoof-shake routine. "Franklin, you might have a future in this business."

Franklin honked once and then, with perfect timing, noticed that the pink lemonade pitcher was running low. He honked twice more and looked pointedly at Eddie, clearly communicating that inventory needed to be replenished.

"He's managing our supply chain now," Frankie observed.

Donald made a note in his operational log: "Franklin demonstrates natural understanding of inventory management and customer flow optimization."

By five o'clock, when they closed for the day, Donald's lemonade enterprise had generated seven dollars and thirty cents in revenue, plus an additional two dollars and fifteen cents in tips that Franklin had personally earned through customer interaction.

After paying back his mother's five-dollar loan plus the promised fifty cents interest, Donald had four dollars and forty-five cents in profit to split among the three human partners. More importantly, he had a business model that actually worked and a pig who was turning out to be the best employee he'd ever had.

"Tomorrow," Donald announced as they cleaned up the operation and packed Franklin's quality control supplies, "we implement Phase Two of the expansion strategy."

"What's Phase Two?" Eddie asked.

"Multiple flavours, extended hours, and advanced Franklin integration," Donald replied. "We're going to build on today's success and create something the neighbourhood has never seen before."

Franklin, apparently understanding that plans were being made, honked his approval and trotted back toward his pen with the satisfied air of someone who'd put in a good day's work.

As Donald counted the day's profits and planned tomorrow's improvements, he felt the kind of confidence that came from genuine success. The garage sale had been chaos, but the lemonade operation was proving that he could actually run a business when he applied proper planning and professional standards.

Of course, he didn't yet know about the Feinberg twins' weekend preparation activities, or their plans for a Monday launch that would feature not only home delivery but also what they were calling "advanced customer service protocols."

But that was Monday's problem. Tonight, Donald had nearly five dollars in profit, a pig with proven business instincts, and a summer full of entrepreneurial possibilities stretching ahead of him.

Franklin honked goodnight from his pen, and Donald fell asleep planning the lemonade empire that was going to make him the most successful fifteen-year-old entrepreneur in Queens.

He still had no idea that the real competition was just getting started.

The Pool Party Pyramid

The lemonade business had been running successfully for exactly six days when Donald discovered that the Feinberg twins weren't just planning to compete, they were planning to annihilate him.

It started on Monday morning when Donald arrived at his usual setup location to find a handwritten note taped to the sidewalk where Station One normally went. The note was written in the twins' distinctive matching handwriting and contained a simple message: "FEINBERG PREMIUM BEVERAGES - HOME DELIVERY NOW AVAILABLE - CALL MAYFAIR 4-7829."

"They're not even open yet and they're already stealing our customers," Eddie pointed out, examining the note while Franklin investigated it with professional interest.

"It's not stealing if they're offering better service," Donald replied, though his voice lacked its usual confidence. "It's just... competitive market positioning."

But as they set up their tables and prepared for another day of what Donald had started calling "neighbourhood beverage leadership," it became clear that the twins' strategy was more sophisticated than simple home delivery.

Mrs. Patterson walked by at nine-fifteen, heading toward the bus stop, and waved at their operation. "Good morning, boys! I won't be stopping today, I've already got a pitcher of lemonade being delivered this afternoon. Very convenient!"

Ten minutes later, Mr. Kowalski passed by with his morning newspaper and called out, "Great pig you've got there! I ordered a half-gallon of that pink stuff from the Feinberg girls. Comes with free ice and everything!"

By ten o'clock, Donald had served exactly three customers, all of whom mentioned that they'd heard about "the new delivery service" and were planning to try it later in the week.

"They're not just competing with us," Donald realized with growing alarm. "They're changing the entire business model. Making us look outdated."

Franklin, sensing the tension in Donald's voice, honked supportively and performed his sitting trick without being asked.

"We need to pivot," Donald announced, using a business term he'd learned from his father's magazines. "If they're going to compete on convenience, we need to compete on experience."

"What kind of experience?" Frankie asked.

Donald looked at their lemonade setup, then at Franklin, then at the spacious Trump backyard with its above-ground swimming pool that his father had installed the previous summer. An idea began forming, the kind of ambitious, slightly dangerous idea that Donald recognized as either genius or catastrophe.

"Pool party," he said slowly. "We're not just selling lemonade anymore. We're selling entertainment. Social experiences. Premium summer recreation that you can't get delivered to your door."

Eddie immediately looked suspicious. "Donald, your parents said no more business ventures that involve the house or Franklin without explicit permission."

"This isn't a business venture," Donald replied, his enthusiasm building as the concept developed. "This is a social event that happens to include refreshment services. Completely different category."

The plan, as Donald explained it over the next hour, was elegantly simple. Instead of competing with the twins' delivery service, they would create an exclusive pool party experience that combined swimming, games, premium beverages, and Franklin's proven entertainment value. Customers wouldn't just buy lemonade, they'd purchase admission to the most sophisticated social event the neighbourhood had ever seen.

"It's experiential retail," Donald explained, sketching diagrams in his notebook. "People don't just want products anymore. They want memories. Experiences they can't get anywhere else."

"How much would we charge for this experience?" Frankie asked.

"Tiered pricing structure," Donald replied. "Basic admission includes pool access and standard lemonade, fifty cents. Premium admission adds games, premium beverages, and Franklin interaction, seventy-five cents. VIP experience includes all of the above plus custom food service and reserved seating, one dollar."

Eddie calculated quickly. "If we get twenty kids to pay an average of seventy-five cents each, that's fifteen dollars. Split three ways, that's five dollars each. Plus, whatever we make on additional beverage sales."

Donald nodded enthusiastically. "And that's just our opening event. Once word spreads about the quality of our pool party experience, we can schedule regular events throughout the summer. Maybe even expand to different themes, Hawaiian luau, Western barbecue, sophisticated cocktail party ambiance."

The more Donald talked about his pool party concept, the more convinced he became that this was the answer to the Feinberg twins' competitive challenge. Home delivery was convenient, but it wasn't fun. People wanted social experiences, especially during summer vacation. A pool party with Franklin as the entertainment coordinator was exactly the kind of unique offering that would establish market differentiation.

The first challenge was securing parental approval for the use of family facilities.

Donald approached this negotiation with the careful strategy he'd developed over the previous week. He waited until his parents were in good moods (Tuesday evening, after his father had received what appeared to be positive news in the mail), dressed in his most responsible clothes, and prepared a presentation that emphasized the social and educational benefits of his proposal.

"Mom, Dad," he said, joining them in the living room after dinner. "I've been thinking about ways to continue learning about business and customer service, and I've developed what I think is a really constructive idea."

Fred Trump looked up from his newspaper. Since the golf club's incident, Donald's father had been observing his son's entrepreneurial activities with mixture of amusement and wariness.

"What kind of idea?" Mrs. Trump asked.

"A neighbourhood social event," Donald said carefully. "Something that would bring the community together while giving me practical experience in event planning and hospitality management."

This was true, technically. It was also a diplomatic way of describing a pool party without immediately mentioning the commercial aspects.

"What kind of social event?" his father asked.

"A pool party. This Saturday afternoon. I'd invite maybe fifteen or twenty kids from the neighbourhood, provide refreshments and entertainment, and practice the kind of social hosting skills that I'll need as an adult."

Donald had rehearsed this presentation, and he was hitting all the right notes, community building, skill development, responsible social activity.

"Would this be a free event?" Mrs. Trump asked, apparently sensing that there were additional layers to her son's proposal.

"Well," Donald said, "I thought it might be appropriate to ask guests to contribute toward refreshment costs. Nothing major, just enough to cover lemonade and snacks. Maybe fifty cents per person."

"Fifty cents?" his father said. "Donald, that sounds less like a social event and more like a business venture."

Donald had anticipated this objection. "It's cost-sharing," he explained. "When adults have dinner parties, everyone contributes something, food, wine, dessert. This is the same principle, just scaled for teenage social activities."

Fred and Mary Trump exchanged looks that Donald couldn't interpret.

"What about Franklin?" Mrs. Trump asked. "Would he be part of this social event?"

"Franklin would provide entertainment," Donald said. "He's very popular with the neighbourhood kids, and he's learned to be much more professional about customer interaction."

This was mostly true. Franklin had indeed become more professional, though his definition of professional customer service sometimes included activities that adults found concerning.

"Franklin stays in his pen," Fred Trump said firmly. "If you're having a pool party, I don't want a pig wandering around unsupervised near water and a crowd of children."

Donald felt his first major compromise coming. Franklin was a key component of his experiential retail strategy, but parental approval was necessary for the use of family facilities.

"Franklin could supervise from his pen," Donald suggested. "Visible entertainment without direct pool interaction."

His parents considered this for several minutes while Donald tried to project responsibility and mature planning.

"Saturday afternoon," Mrs. Trump said finally. "Two to five o'clock. Maximum twenty guests. You're responsible for cleanup and any damages. And if this turns into anything like the garage sale situation, there won't be any more social events this summer."

"Understood," Donald said. "This is going to be the most organized and responsible social event you've ever seen."

Wednesday and Thursday were spent in intensive party planning. Donald created guest lists, developed activity schedules, and designed what he called "premium hospitality protocols." He also spent considerable time training Franklin in what he hoped would be appropriate party behaviour.

"The key," Donald explained to Franklin during one of their training sessions, "is controlled entertainment. You're the star attraction, but you stay in your designated area and let the party come to you. No independent community outreach initiatives."

Franklin honked acknowledgment and performed his sitting trick, which Donald took as agreement to the new operational parameters.

Eddie and Frankie were assigned specific party management responsibilities. Eddie would handle beverage service and maintain the premium lemonade standards they'd established during the week. Frankie would coordinate games and activities, ensuring that guests remained entertained and engaged throughout the event.

"What's your role?" Eddie asked during Thursday's planning session.

"Party host and overall experience director," Donald replied. "I'll handle guest relations, manage the premium service delivery, and ensure that everyone has the kind of social experience they'll remember and recommend to their friends."

The guest list had grown during the planning process. Donald had started with fifteen confirmed attendees but had expanded to twenty-three after several neighbourhood kids heard about the party and specifically requested invitations. This meant more potential revenue, but also more complexity in terms of logistics and crowd management.

"Twenty-three guests at fifty cents each is eleven-fifty in admission fees," Donald calculated. "Plus, additional beverage sales, plus tips for premium service. We could clear fifteen dollars easy."

"What if people don't want to pay?" Frankie asked.

"They'll pay," Donald said confidently. "Once they see the quality of the experience we're providing, fifty cents will seem like a bargain. This is going to be the party everyone talks about for the rest of the summer."

Saturday morning dawned hot and humid, perfect pool party weather. Donald spent the early hours preparing what he called "venue management", setting up the backyard for optimal guest flow, arranging seating areas around the pool, and creating designated zones for different activities.

He'd borrowed additional tables from the basement and covered them with tablecloths appropriated from his mother's linen closet. The lemonade service area was positioned for easy access but away from the pool to prevent beverage contamination from splashing. Franklin's pen had been decorated with streamers and positioned where he could observe and interact with guests without direct access to the party area.

"This looks pretty professional," Eddie admitted as they completed the setup.

"It looks like a real party," Frankie added, arranging the final details of the games area.

Donald surveyed their work with satisfaction. The backyard had been transformed from ordinary family space into what could genuinely be called a premium social venue. Tables were positioned at optimal angles, the pool area was clear and inviting, and Franklin was already greeting early arriving guests with his signature combination of dignity and charm.

The first guests arrived at exactly two o'clock, the Kowalski twins, followed closely by several kids from Donald's school and a few younger children from the neighbourhood. Donald greeted each arrival with his most professional hosting manner.

"Welcome to the Trump Premium Pool Party Experience!" he announced as each guest arrived. "Admission includes unlimited pool access, premium lemonade service, organized entertainment activities, and interaction with Franklin Roosevelt, our celebrity pig. That's fifty cents per person, payable to Frankie at the admission table."

Most guests paid without question, clearly excited about the pool and curious about Franklin's role in the festivities. A few asked about the admission fee, but Donald had prepared responses that emphasized the exclusive nature of the experience and the quality of services included.

"This is like a real party," said Mary Flynn, handing over her fifty cents. "With actual party planning and everything."

Donald felt a surge of pride. This was exactly the kind of sophisticated social event that demonstrated real organizational skills and business thinking.

The first hour went smoothly. Guests rotated between swimming, games, and Franklin observation in a natural flow that Donald recognized as successful crowd management. Eddie kept the lemonade service running efficiently, offering both classic and premium varieties with the professional presentation they'd perfected during the week.

Franklin, contained but visible, was performing his role as party entertainment with obvious enjoyment. He greeted guests who approached his pen, performed tricks on request, and occasionally honked commentary on the pool activities that everyone found amusing.

"Your pig is the best part of this party," Lisa Chen told Donald when she arrived at two-thirty with a group of friends from the next block.

Donald felt his usual tongue-tied reaction to Lisa's attention, but this time he had a successful party happening around him, which gave him confidence. "Franklin's got natural party instincts," he managed. "He understands social dynamics."

"Can I give him some lemonade?" Lisa asked.

"Franklin has his own beverage service area," Donald replied, indicating a special bucket of water that he'd positioned next to the pig pen. "He maintains professional boundaries during social events."

This wasn't entirely true, Franklin clearly wanted to be more directly involved in the party activities, but Donald had learned from previous experience that Franklin's direct participation could lead to complications.

The trouble started when the party was at its peak success. By three o'clock, Donald had twenty-one guests enjoying the pool, consuming premium beverages, and generating the kind of positive social energy that he recognized as successful event management.

That's when Tommy Kowalski, the six-year-old whose attention span had been thoroughly occupied by Franklin's entertainment, decided that the party would be even better if Franklin could actually swim with everyone else.

"Why can't Franklin come in the pool?" Tommy asked loudly enough for the entire party to hear.

Donald felt immediate panic. This was exactly the kind of question that could demine his carefully maintained party management authority.

"Franklin doesn't swim," Donald said quickly. "He's a land-based entertainment specialist."

"But pigs can swim," said Brains Morrison, the smart kid with the pocket protector who always had factual information available at inconvenient times. "I read that pigs are actually excellent swimmers. Better than most farm animals."

This information sparked immediate interest among the party guests, several of whom began discussing the theoretical swimming abilities of pigs while looking expectantly at Franklin.

"Franklin could probably swim really well," agreed Mary Flynn. "He's so smart about everything else."

Donald realized that he was facing a potential party crisis. The guests were becoming fixated on Franklin's swimming potential, and their current entertainment was losing appeal by comparison.

"Franklin's swimming abilities aren't really relevant to today's party activities," Donald said, trying to redirect attention back to the organized entertainment he'd planned.

But Franklin had been listening to the conversation with obvious interest, and he apparently had opinions about his swimming potential. He began honking in a pattern that Donald had learned meant he wanted attention, and when the party guests gathered around his pen, Franklin performed an elaborate series of movements that looked suspiciously like swimming motions.

"He wants to swim!" Tommy declared. "Look, he's showing us he knows how!"

The crowd of children began chanting "Franklin! Franklin! Franklin!" while the pig performed increasingly dramatic demonstrations of his theoretical swimming technique.

Donald found himself facing the kind of leadership challenge that separated professional event managers from amateurs. His guests wanted something that was outside the planned party parameters, but denying their request could result in decreased satisfaction and negative word-of-mouth.

"Tell you what," Donald said, making the kind of executive decision that he'd read about in business magazines. "Franklin can demonstrate his swimming abilities, but we need to maintain safety protocols and proper supervision."

This seemed like a reasonable compromise, but Donald immediately realized that he had no idea how to safely introduce a pig to swimming activities. Franklin was clearly eager to participate, the party guests were excited about the prospect, and Donald's parents had specifically forbidden unsupervised pig activities near the pool.

"Maybe Franklin could just put his feet in the water?" suggested Lisa, apparently sensing Donald's dilemma. "Like testing the temperature?"

This seemed manageable. Donald opened Franklin's pen and led him to the edge of the pool while the party guests gathered around to watch. Franklin approached the water with obvious curiosity and carefully extended one hoof to test the temperature.

The pool water was perfectly warm, and Franklin apparently found it acceptable because he immediately waded in up to his knees, honking with what could only be described as delight.

"Franklin likes it!" several children announced simultaneously.

Franklin, encouraged by the positive audience response, waded deeper into the pool until the water reached his belly. Then he began moving through the water with the natural paddling motion that proved Brains Morrison had been correct about pigs' swimming abilities.

The party guests were absolutely delighted. Franklin swimming was apparently the most entertaining thing they'd ever seen, and Donald found himself watching twenty-one children cheer enthusiastically for his pig's aquatic abilities.

"This is the best party ever!" Mary Flynn declared, and several other guests agreed loudly.

Donald felt a moment of pure triumph. He'd successfully adapted to unexpected guest requests, delivered entertainment that exceeded expectations, and created what was clearly a memorable social experience.

Then Franklin discovered that he could dive.

It started when Tommy Kowalski threw a pool toy into the deep end and jokingly asked if Franklin could retrieve it. Franklin, apparently taking this as a legitimate challenge, paddled over to investigate the toy's location.

What happened next exceeded everyone's expectations, including Franklin's.

Franklin took a deep breath, disappeared completely underwater, and emerged thirty seconds later with the pool toy clenched firmly in his teeth. He paddled back to the shallow end and deposited the toy at the edge of the pool while the party guests exploded into applause.

"Franklin can dive!" someone shouted.

"He's like a pig submarine!" added someone else.

Franklin, clearly pleased with his reception, honked triumphantly and looked around for additional diving challenges.

Donald realized that Franklin's swimming abilities were rapidly becoming the primary entertainment focus of the party, which was both good and potentially problematic. The guests were having more fun than he'd imagined possible, but Franklin's aquatic adventures were creating logistical complications.

"Franklin!" Donald called out. "That was excellent diving, but maybe we should return to land-based party activities!"

Franklin ignored this suggestion and began investigating the pool's filtration system with the same systematic curiosity he'd applied to previous business ventures.

"Donald," Eddie said quietly, "maybe we should get him out of the pool before he breaks something?"

But the party guests were having too much fun watching Franklin's aquatic explorations to support any plan that involved ending the swimming exhibition. They began making requests for specific diving demonstrations and asking if Franklin could perform underwater tricks.

Franklin, clearly enjoying his role as aquatic entertainer, began showing off. He swam laps around the pool, dove for additional toys, and discovered that he could float on his back while honking, which the crowd found absolutely hilarious.

Donald tried to maintain party management control, but Franklin had clearly taken over as entertainment director. The guests were more interested in pig swimming than in the organized activities Donald had planned, and Franklin was obviously having more fun than anyone else at the party.

"This is amazing," Lisa said, approaching Donald while Franklin demonstrated his backstroke technique. "How did you know Franklin could swim like that?"

"Strategic entertainment planning," Donald replied, though he'd had no idea Franklin possessed aquatic abilities. "I always research all available party resources before finalizing the event design."

This was a complete lie, but it sounded professional, and Lisa seemed impressed by Donald's apparent depth of planning.

The party continued successfully for another hour, with Franklin providing swimming entertainment while Donald managed refreshment service and guest relations. They'd sold additional lemonade, several guests had upgraded to premium admission levels, and Donald was calculating record-breaking profit margins.

Then Franklin discovered the pool filter intake.

The above-ground pool had a filtration system that drew water through a small opening near the bottom of the pool wall. Franklin, in his systematic exploration of pool infrastructure, had noticed the gentle current created by the intake and decided to investigate its operational mechanics.

What Franklin found was that if he positioned himself correctly near the intake, the water flow created a pleasant massage effect against his considerable bulk. Franklin settled into position and began honking with obvious satisfaction.

This blocked the filter intake completely.

"Donald," Eddie said urgently, "the pool pump is making weird noises."

Donald looked at the pool equipment and saw that the filtration system was struggling to maintain proper water circulation with Franklin positioned directly against the intake. The pump was working harder than usual, and Donald could hear mechanical sounds that suggested potential equipment stress.

"Franklin!" Donald called out. "You need to move away from the pool machinery!"

But Franklin had discovered the perfect aquatic massage position and wasn't interested in relocating. He honked contentedly and settled more firmly against the intake, completely blocking water flow to the filtration system.

The pump made a grinding noise that Donald was pretty sure wasn't normal.

"Everyone out of the pool!" Donald announced, making another executive decision. "We're taking a brief swimming break for equipment maintenance!"

This resulted in twenty-one disappointed party guests climbing out of the pool while Franklin continued to enjoy his mechanical massage, apparently unaware that he was causing a technical crisis.

"Franklin," Donald said, approaching the pig in the water, "you need to cooperate with pool safety protocols."

Franklin looked at Donald and honked what sounded like disagreement.

Donald realized that removing Franklin from his preferred pool position was going to require either negotiation or physical intervention, neither of which he was confident about attempting in front of his entire party guest list.

"Maybe we could offer Franklin an alternative relaxation area?" Lisa suggested helpfully.

Donald looked around the backyard for something that might appeal to Franklin more than his current aquatic massage position. The only option that seemed comparable was the garden hose, which his mother used for watering plants and which had adjustable pressure settings.

"Franklin," Donald called out, "would you be interested in premium spa services on dry land?"

He turned on the garden hose and adjusted it to create a gentle spray that approximated the pool filter's massage effect. Franklin watched this demonstration with obvious interest, apparently recognizing that this might be an acceptable alternative to his current position.

After several minutes of negotiation, which mostly involved Donald describing the benefits of hose-based spa treatment while Franklin weighed his options, Franklin finally paddled away from the filter intake and climbed out of the pool to investigate the garden hose alternative.

The pool pump immediately resumed normal operation, and the party guests cheered Franklin's cooperation while he settled into position for his new spa treatment.

"Crisis management," Donald announced to his guests, trying to turn the technical difficulty into evidence of his party planning competence. "Part of premium event hosting is adapting to unexpected situations while maintaining guest satisfaction."

The party continued for another hour, with Franklin enjoying his garden hose spa while the guests returned to swimming and lemonade consumption. Donald felt that he'd successfully handled a potentially serious operational crisis while maintaining party momentum and guest satisfaction.

But Franklin's spa treatment had attracted additional attention from the neighbourhood. Several adults had stopped by to see what was happening in the Trump backyard, and word was spreading about "the pool party with the swimming pig."

"Donald," Mrs. Rodriguez called over the fence, "is that pig supposed to be playing in your garden hose?"

"Franklin's receiving professional spa treatment," Donald replied. "It's part of our comprehensive party entertainment package."

Mrs. Rodriguez looked sceptical but didn't pursue the issue further.

The real problem developed when Franklin finished his spa session and decided that he wanted to return to swimming. But instead of going back to the pool, Franklin apparently concluded that the garden hose had been merely a warm-up for more extensive aquatic activities.

Franklin trotted across the backyard, past the pool where the party guests were swimming, and headed directly for the fence that separated the Trump property from the Hendersons' yard.

"Franklin," Donald called out in alarm, "the party is happening over here!"

But Franklin had spotted something that interested him more than party hosting: the Hendersons had installed a small decorative pond in their backyard, complete with lily pads and what appeared to be several goldfish.

Franklin squeezed under the fence with the ease of previous escapes and approached the Henderson pond with obvious enthusiasm. The pond was smaller than the pool but apparently met Franklin's standards for aquatic recreation because he immediately waded in and began exploring the lily pad arrangements.

"WHAT IS THAT PIG DOING IN MY POND?" Mrs. Henderson's voice carried clearly over the fence.

Donald's party guests, hearing the commotion, climbed out of the pool to see what was happening. They clustered around the fence and began cheering as Franklin conducted his exploration of the Henderson aquatic facilities.

"Franklin's expanding his swimming venue," Donald announced, trying to maintain party host authority while internally panicking about neighbourhood relations. "He's demonstrating advanced aquatic adaptability!"

Mrs. Henderson appeared in her back door holding what looked like a garden hose of her own. "GET THAT PIG OUT OF MY POND!"

Franklin, apparently interpreting Mrs. Henderson's shouting as encouragement, began performing his diving routine in the pond. This was considerably more challenging in the shallow water, but Franklin adapted by creating elaborate splashing displays that sent water in all directions.

The party guests were absolutely delighted by Franklin's pond performance, but Donald could see Mrs. Henderson advancing across her backyard with obvious hostile intent.

"Franklin!" Donald called out desperately. "Customer service emergency! We need you back at party headquarters!"

But Franklin was having too much fun exploring the Henderson pond ecosystem to respond to administrative requests. He'd discovered the goldfish and was attempting to engage them in the same diplomatic relations he'd established with neighbourhood dogs.

The goldfish were considerably less cooperative than dogs had been.

"Everyone back to our pool!" Donald announced to his party guests. "Franklin's just conducting quality research on alternative aquatic venues! Resume party activities!"

This worked for about five minutes, until Mrs. Henderson turned on her garden hose and began directing a stream of water toward Franklin with obvious intention to encourage his departure.

Franklin, however, interpreted the garden hose as an invitation to enhanced spa treatment. Instead of leaving the pond, he positioned himself to receive the full benefit of Mrs. Henderson's water stream while continuing his goldfish diplomacy efforts.

"Mrs. Henderson!" Donald called over the fence. "Franklin's just expressing appreciation for your beautiful pond! He'll be returning to our party venue shortly!"

Mrs. Henderson's response suggested that she was not interested in Franklin's aesthetic appreciation or his timeline for departure.

Donald realized that he needed to take direct action before the situation escalated beyond his party management capabilities. He climbed over the fence, adding another set of tears to his party hosting outfit, and approached Franklin in the pond.

"Franklin," he said quietly, "you're compromising our neighbourhood relations and potentially threatening our future event hosting opportunities."

Franklin looked at Donald and then at Mrs. Henderson, who was maintaining her garden hose offensive while making comments about property rights and livestock control.

"If you come back to our party right now," Donald continued, "I'll personally ensure that you get premium spa treatment for the rest of the afternoon."

Franklin considered this offer while a goldfish swam directly between his front legs. Then, with the dignity of someone who'd made an important business decision, Franklin waded out of the pond and trotted back toward the fence.

Getting Franklin back over the fence required the assistance of three party guests and a good deal of careful manoeuvring, but within ten minutes, Franklin was back in the Trump backyard receiving enthusiastic applause from the party attendees.

"Franklin's return from his aquatic research expedition!" Donald announced, turning the pond incident into planned entertainment. "He's now ready to continue providing premium party services!"

The party concluded at five o'clock with what Donald considered tremendous success. Twenty-one guests had attended (two had to leave early for family obligations), admission fees had generated ten dollars and fifty cents, additional lemonade sales added three dollars and twenty cents, and tips for Franklin's entertainment had contributed another one dollar and forty cents.

After expenses (lemons, sugar, pool chemicals, and fifty cents for Mrs. Henderson's garden damage), Donald calculated a net profit of twelve dollars and thirty cents, which split three ways meant over four dollars each.

"That's the most money I've ever made in one day," Frankie said as they counted the final receipts.

"That's the most money I've ever made in one week," Eddie added.

Donald felt the satisfaction that came from successful event management and profitable business operations. "This is just the beginning," he said. "Once word spreads about the quality of our party experiences, we'll have people requesting premium social events all summer long."

Franklin, exhausted from his dual role as swimming entertainer and pond explorer, honked agreement and settled down for a well-deserved nap.

As Donald cleaned up the party area and calculated plans for future events, he felt confident that he'd found the perfect answer to the Feinberg twins' competitive challenge. Home delivery was convenient, but it couldn't compete with the kind of memorable social experiences that featured swimming pigs and premium hospitality.

Of course, he didn't yet know that Mrs. Henderson had spent the evening calling other neighbours to discuss "the pig situation" and that several parents were beginning to question the supervision standards at Trump family social events.

But that was tomorrow's challenge. Tonight, Donald had over four dollars in profit, a pig with proven party hosting abilities, and a summer full of social event possibilities stretching ahead of him.

Franklin honked goodnight from his pen, and Donald fell asleep planning the luau party that would feature not only premium beverages but also what he was calling "authentic Pacific Island entertainment experiences."

He still had no idea that the real competition was about to escalate beyond anything he'd imagined possible.

The Water Balloon Arms Race

The pool party had been such a tremendous success that by Monday morning, Donald was fielding requests for three additional social events and had received what he considered a significant business opportunity from an unexpected source.

Mrs. Chen had called on Sunday evening to ask if Donald might be interested in providing "entertainment services" for her daughter Lisa's birthday party the following weekend. The conversation had been brief but professional, and Donald had hung up the phone feeling like he'd just landed his first major corporate contract.

"She specifically requested Franklin," Donald told Eddie and Frankie as they conducted their weekly business planning session in the backyard. "Lisa's mom said the swimming pig was the most creative party entertainment she'd ever seen. This could be our breakthrough into the premium private event market."

Franklin, hearing his name mentioned, honked approvingly from his pen and performed his sitting trick for emphasis.

"How much do we charge for private party services?" Frankie asked.

Donald consulted his notebook, where he'd been developing pricing strategies for expanded business offerings. "Premium private event coordination should command premium pricing. I'm thinking five dollars for basic entertainment package, eight dollars for full aquatic demonstration, and ten dollars for what we could call the 'Franklin Deluxe Experience.'"

"Ten dollars?" Eddie said. "Donald, that's more money than most kids see in a month."

"That's exactly why it's premium pricing," Donald replied. "We're not competing in the mass market anymore. We're positioning ourselves as the exclusive provider of unique entertainment experiences that you literally cannot get anywhere else in Queens."

This was, Donald felt, sound business logic. Franklin's combination of natural charm, aquatic abilities, and social intelligence was genuinely unique. If they were going to commercialize Franklin's talents, they should price them according to their true market value.

The problem was that word of Franklin's swimming abilities had spread beyond potential customers. On Monday afternoon, while Donald was planning Lisa's birthday party logistics, Eddie came running across the backyard with news that changed everything.

"Donald," Eddie said breathlessly, "you need to see what's happening on Elm Street."

Donald followed Eddie to the front yard, where they had a clear view of the next block. What Donald saw made his stomach drop.

The Feinberg twins had set up what could only be described as a military operation.

They had four tables arranged in precise formation, each staffed by a different neighbourhood kid wearing matching t shirts that read "FEINBERG DELIVERY SERVICES." They had actual glass pitchers instead of plastic ones, professional-looking signs with hand-lettered pricing, and what appeared to be a sophisticated ordering and dispatch system.

But most concerning of all, they had a bicycle brigade.

"Six kids with bikes," Eddie reported. "Taking orders, delivering to houses, collecting payment. They're covering a twelve-block radius. And they're not just selling lemonade anymore."

Donald watched in growing alarm as the Feinberg operation handled what appeared to be steady customer traffic. Kids on bicycles were arriving with empty bags and leaving with loaded delivery baskets. Orders were being taken, money was changing hands, and the entire operation was running with the kind of efficiency that Donald recognized as serious competition.

"What else are they selling?" Donald asked.

"Ice cream sandwiches, popsicles, comic books, and something called 'premium snack packages,'" Eddie said. "Plus, they're taking advance orders for birthday party supplies and custom entertainment services."

"Custom entertainment services?" Donald felt a chill that had nothing to do with the afternoon breeze.

"Josephine was telling Mrs. Patterson about their 'professional party planning services with guaranteed satisfaction.' Madeline was showing her a photo album of previous events they've organized."

Donald stared at the Feinberg operation and realized that his competition wasn't just trying to steal his lemonade customers, they were systematically targeting his entire business model. Private parties, premium services, exclusive entertainment, everything Donald had been building was being directly challenged by an operation that appeared to be better organized, more efficient, and significantly more professional.

"They've been planning this for weeks," Donald said with growing recognition. "Ever since they saw our first lemonade stand. They've been developing a complete competitive response strategy."

Franklin, sensing the tension in Donald's voice, approached the fence and honked what sounded like a question.

"Franklin wants to know what the problem is," Frankie translated.

Donald looked at his pig, who'd been the key to every successful venture they'd attempted, and felt the kind of strategic clarity that came in moments of genuine crisis.

"The problem," Donald said slowly, "is that we've been thinking too small. The Feinbergs are competing on efficiency and scale, but they don't have anything that can match Franklin's unique entertainment value. We need to leverage our competitive advantages while they're still establishing market position."

"What kind of competitive advantages?" Eddie asked.

Donald's mind was racing through possibilities. The Feinbergs had organization and delivery logistics, but they didn't have a swimming pig. They had professional presentation, but they didn't have Franklin's proven crowd appeal. They had efficiency, but they didn't have the kind of memorable entertainment that created customer loyalty.

"Water balloon warfare," Donald announced.

Eddie and Frankie stared at him.

"Think about it," Donald continued, his enthusiasm building as the concept developed. "Summer entertainment, organized competition, teams and strategy and victory conditions. We provide the balloons, the playing field, the rules, and the coordination. Franklin serves as neutral referee and entertainment during breaks."

"You want to organize water balloon fights?" Eddie asked.

"I want to revolutionize summer recreation," Donald corrected. "Turn random neighbourhood water balloon chaos into structured, competitive entertainment that families will pay for. Premium recreational experiences with professional organization and guaranteed fun."

The more Donald thought about his water balloon warfare concept, the more convinced he became that this was the perfect response to the Feinberg twins' systematic approach. Home delivery was convenient, but it wasn't exciting. Professional efficiency was impressive, but it wasn't fun. Water balloon warfare with Franklin as referee was both unique and irresistibly entertaining.

"How much would we charge for water balloon warfare?" Frankie asked.

"Tiered participation structure," Donald replied, pulling out his notebook to sketch organizational diagrams. "Basic combat admission, twenty-five cents for balloon allocation and battlefield access. Premium warfare package, fifty cents for additional ammunition and strategic consultation. Deluxe military experience, seventy-five cents for all of the above plus Franklin interaction and victory ceremony participation."

Donald spent Tuesday morning developing what he called "comprehensive warfare protocols." Teams would be organized by age and experience level to ensure fair competition. Battlefield boundaries would be clearly marked using rope and stakes borrowed from his father's garage. Rules of engagement would emphasize safety while maximizing entertainment value.

Most importantly, Franklin would serve as neutral referee, ensuring fair play while providing entertainment during strategic planning breaks.

"Franklin's natural authority will prevent disputes," Donald explained to Eddie and Frankie during Tuesday's planning session. "Nobody's going to argue with a pig about rule violations."

Wednesday was devoted to what Donald called "operational preparation and marketing outreach." He created hand-lettered signs advertising "TRUMP'S WATER BALLOON WARFARE - SATURDAY 10 AM - PROFESSIONAL COMPETITION - FRANKLIN ROOSEVELT OFFICIATING." He also went door-to-door throughout the neighbourhood, personally inviting potential participants and explaining the competitive advantages of organized water balloon combat over amateur backyard chaos.

"It's like regular water balloon fights," Donald explained to Mrs. Patterson, "but with actual rules, fair teams, and professional supervision. No arguments about who hit who first, no disputes about boundary violations, no chaos. Just pure strategic summer entertainment."

Mrs. Patterson seemed intrigued by the concept of organized water balloon activities. "And Franklin will be supervising?"

"Franklin will serve as head referee," Donald confirmed. "He's got natural authority and excellent judgment about fair play. Plus, he provides entertainment value during strategic planning breaks."

By Thursday evening, Donald had fifteen confirmed participants and several adults who'd expressed interest in observing the competition. More importantly, he'd calculated potential revenues that exceeded anything he'd generated from previous ventures.

"Fifteen participants at an average of fifty cents each is seven-fifty in admission fees," Donald told his parents during Thursday dinner, carefully presenting his water balloon warfare as responsible recreational planning rather than commercial enterprise. "Plus, refreshment sales and tips for Franklin's officiating services. This could be our most successful community event yet."

Fred Trump looked up from his meatloaf. "Donald, this sounds like you're charging neighbourhood kids to have water balloon fights in our backyard."

"I'm providing structure and organization for recreational activities that would happen anyway," Donald replied. "Professional supervision, safety protocols, and fair competition standards. Parents appreciate knowing that their children are participating in properly managed entertainment rather than random neighbourhood chaos."

This was diplomatically phrased, but it was also mostly accurate. Donald had learned from previous ventures that parents valued organization and supervision, especially when it involved activities that could potentially result in property damage or neighbourhood disputes.

"What about cleanup?" Mrs. Trump asked.

"Complete post-event restoration included in the service package," Donald promised. "Part of professional event management is leaving the venue in better condition than we found it."

His parents exchanged looks that Donald had learned to interpret as cautious approval mixed with anticipatory concern.

"Saturday morning only," Fred Trump said finally. "Ten to noon. And if there are any complaints from neighbours or any property damage, this will be the last organized event of the summer."

"Understood," Donald said. "This is going to be the most professional and responsible water balloon competition you've ever seen."

Friday was spent in final preparations and what Donald called "equipment procurement and battlefield engineering." This mostly involved filling several hundred water balloons using the garden hose, arranging them in tactical supply stations around the backyard, and marking battlefield boundaries with rope and wooden stakes.

Donald had also borrowed military strategy books from the library and developed what he considered sophisticated team organization and victory condition protocols. Teams would be balanced for fairness, battles would be timed for optimal pacing, and Franklin would maintain neutral authority throughout the competition.

"Franklin," Donald explained during Friday evening's final planning session, "your role tomorrow is crucial. You're not just entertainment, you're the authority figure who ensures fair play and maintains competitive integrity."

Franklin honked acknowledgment and performed his sitting trick, which Donald interpreted as understanding of the responsibilities involved.

Saturday morning dawned clear and hot, perfect water balloon weather. Donald spent the early hours completing battlefield preparation and reviewing his operational protocols. By nine-thirty, everything was ready for what he expected would be the most successful recreational event of the summer.

The first participants arrived at exactly ten o'clock. Tommy Kowalski and his twin brother, followed by several kids from Donald's school and a few younger children from the neighbourhood. Donald greeted each arrival with his most professional event coordination manner.

"Welcome to Trump's Water Balloon Warfare Championship!" he announced as each participant arrived. "Today's competition features strategic team-based combat, professional refereeing by Franklin Roosevelt, and victory ceremonies with prizes for outstanding performance. Admission is fifty cents per participant, payable to Eddie at the registration table."

Most participants paid enthusiastically, clearly excited about the prospect of organized water balloon combat. Donald felt confident that his pricing strategy was appropriate and that the quality of experience would justify the premium cost.

Franklin had been positioned at the centre of the battlefield, where he could observe all combat activities and intervene if referee decisions were needed. He was wearing a small flag tied around his neck that Donald had designed to indicate his neutral authority status.

"Franklin will ensure fair play throughout the competition," Donald explained to the assembled participants. "His decisions are final, and arguing with the referee results in immediate disqualification."

Franklin honked officially and performed his sitting trick, establishing his authority with the crowd.

The first round of combat went smoothly. Donald had organized teams of four participants each, balanced for age and experience, with clearly defined objectives and time limits. Franklin patrolled the battlefield boundaries, occasionally honking when participants attempted to cross established lines or violate ammunition allocation rules.

"This is actually really fun," admitted Brains Morrison, who'd been sceptical about paying for water balloon activities but was clearly enjoying the structured competition format.

Donald felt vindicated in his strategic planning. Organized competition was definitely superior to random neighbourhood chaos, and Franklin's referee presence was maintaining order while adding entertainment value.

The problems began when Franklin decided that referee neutrality didn't extend to protecting participants from obviously unfair tactical situations.

During the second round of competition, six-year-old Tommy Kowalski found himself surrounded by three older boys who were clearly planning to eliminate him from the game through overwhelming balloon bombardment. Tommy was standing in the designated safe zone, clutching his remaining ammunition, when Franklin noticed the tactical imbalance.

Instead of maintaining neutral referee position, Franklin trotted directly into the combat zone and positioned himself between Tommy and the advancing opponents. He honked twice, which Donald had established as the signal for cease-fire, and looked pointedly at the older boys.

"Franklin's calling a fairness intervention," Donald announced, though this hadn't been part of his established referee protocols. "Apparently he's identified a tactical imbalance that requires adjustment."

The older boys protested that they were following established rules and that Franklin didn't have authority to intervene in legitimate strategic positioning.

Franklin responded by sitting directly in front of Tommy and refusing to move until the older boys agreed to pursue different targets.

"Your pig's picking favourites," complained one of the older boys.

"Franklin's ensuring competitive balance," Donald replied, though he was beginning to realize that Franklin's concept of fair refereeing might be more complex than simple rule enforcement.

Franklin maintained his protective position until the older boys moved away to engage different opponents. Then he honked approval and returned to his neutral referee location, apparently satisfied with his intervention.

"Franklin's got his own rules," Lisa Chen observed. She'd arrived to watch the competition and was clearly amused by Franklin's independent approach to referee authority.

"Franklin understands the spirit of competition," Donald replied, trying to turn Franklin's unauthorized intervention into evidence of sophisticated officiating. "He's maintaining both rule compliance and competitive fairness."

This explanation satisfied most participants, but Donald was beginning to worry about Franklin's expanding interpretation of his referee responsibilities.

The third round of combat tested Franklin's neutrality even further. During an intense battle between two evenly matched teams, one participant, Mary Flynn, slipped on the wet grass and fell directly into Franklin's water bowl, soaking herself completely and losing all her remaining ammunition.

Franklin immediately honked the cease-fire signal and trotted over to investigate Mary's situation. After determining that she was unhurt but disadvantaged, Franklin began honking in a pattern that Donald had never heard before.

"What's Franklin trying to say?" Mary asked, standing up and dripping water from Franklin's bowl onto the battlefield.

Franklin trotted over to the ammunition supply station, selected a water balloon in his mouth, and carried it back to Mary. Then he performed his sitting trick and looked expectantly at the other participants.

"Franklin's providing replacement ammunition," Donald announced, trying to interpret Franklin's actions as legitimate referee decisions. "He's ensuring that equipment failures don't compromise competitive balance."

This created immediate controversy among the other participants, several of whom pointed out that Franklin was supposed to be neutral and that providing ammunition to specific players was clearly biased officiating.

Franklin responded to this criticism by trotting to the ammunition station and selecting additional balloons for everyone who'd raised objections. Within minutes, he'd personally distributed replacement ammunition to all participants, apparently concluding that the best way to maintain neutrality was to ensure everyone was equally well-armed.

"Franklin's implementing universal supply equity," Donald announced, though he was starting to realize that Franklin's referee methods were becoming more complex than his original organizational structure could accommodate.

The competition continued with Franklin providing ongoing tactical consultation to all participants. When someone ran out of ammunition, Franklin retrieved replacement balloons. When someone slipped or fell, Franklin investigated to ensure they weren't injured. When disputes arose about rule violations, Franklin honked his cease-fire signal and positioned himself between the arguing parties until they resolved their differences.

"Your pig's better at managing kids than most adults," observed Mrs. Chen, who'd arrived to watch her daughter's participation in the competition.

Donald felt proud of Franklin's natural leadership abilities, but he was also beginning to realize that Franklin was rapidly becoming the actual organizer of the water balloon warfare while Donald served as the human who collected admission fees.

The real crisis developed during the championship round, when Donald's carefully planned tournament structure encountered an opponent, he hadn't anticipated: the Feinberg twins.

Madeline and Josephine arrived at eleven-thirty, just as the final competition was beginning. They approached Donald's registration table with the focused attention of military strategists conducting battlefield reconnaissance.

"Interesting concept," Madeline said, surveying the organized chaos of water balloon combat.

"Professional organization," Josephine added, watching Franklin distribute ammunition to participants with obvious efficiency.

"Are you here to participate in the competition?" Donald asked, though he suspected their motives were more complex than simple entertainment.

"We're observing operational effectiveness," Madeline replied.

"Evaluating competitive positioning," Josephine continued.

"Understanding market differentiation strategies," they concluded together.

Donald felt his confidence waver. The twins' synchronized analysis approach always made him feel like he was being professionally evaluated and found wanting.

"The registration fee is fifty cents per participant," Donald said, hoping they would either pay and participate or leave and let him focus on managing the current competition.

"We'll observe today," Madeline said.

"Participate next week," Josephine added.

Then they positioned themselves at the edge of the battlefield and began taking notes in their matching notebooks while Franklin continued his complex referee duties.

Donald tried to focus on managing the championship round, but the twins' presence was distracting. They were clearly developing some kind of competitive response strategy, and their note-taking suggested that they were analysing every aspect of his water balloon warfare operation.

The championship round featured four teams of three participants each, competing in elimination-style combat with Franklin serving as both referee and tactical consultant. The competition was intense, with strategic balloon conservation, coordinated team attacks, and sophisticated defensive positioning that impressed even Donald with its complexity.

Franklin was in his element, honking cease-fire signals when safety issues arose, distributing ammunition when supply imbalances developed, and occasionally performing his sitting trick to defuse tensions between competing teams.

"Franklin's the best referee ever," declared Tommy Kowalski, who'd made it to the championship round despite being the youngest participant.

"Franklin understands fair play," agreed Mary Flynn, who was leading her team with strategic thinking that would have impressed actual military planners.

Donald was feeling triumphant about the success of his organizational structure when Franklin made a referee decision that changed the entire nature of the competition.

During the final battle between the two remaining teams, one participant, Brains Morrison, attempted what Donald considered an obviously illegal tactical manoeuvre. Brains had positioned himself outside the established battlefield boundaries and was lobbing water balloons into the combat zone from what was essentially a neutral territory position.

Franklin noticed this rule violation and honked his cease-fire signal. But instead of simply calling a penalty against Brains, Franklin trotted over to the ammunition station, selected a large balloon, and carried it directly to the opposing team's captain.

Then Franklin positioned himself next to the captain, honked twice, and looked pointedly at Brains's illegal position.

"Franklin's providing tactical consultation to restore competitive balance," Donald announced, though he was beginning to realize that Franklin's referee decisions were becoming increasingly complex and potentially controversial.

Brains protested that Franklin was supposed to be neutral and that providing tactical assistance to opposing teams violated referee ethics.

Franklin responded by trotting over to Brains, honking the cease-fire signal again, and gently but firmly nudging him back into the legal battlefield boundaries.

"Franklin's enforcing boundary compliance," Donald said, though the other participants were beginning to question whether Franklin's referee methods were actually neutral.

The situation escalated when Franklin decided that the best way to ensure fair play was to participate directly in conflict resolution.

When the final battle resumed, both teams immediately targeted each other with concentrated balloon bombardments. The combat was intense and exciting, but it was also generating the kind of competitive tensions that Donald recognized as potentially problematic.

One participant complained that opponents were throwing too hard. Another argued that his team was being unfairly targeted by multiple opponents. A third claimed that ammunition distribution had been unequal from the beginning.

Franklin listened to these complaints with obvious concern. Then, apparently concluding that the best way to resolve competitive disputes was through direct demonstration, Franklin positioned himself in the centre of the battlefield and began honking for attention.

When all participants stopped fighting and looked at Franklin, the pig performed an elaborate demonstration of proper water balloon throwing technique. He picked up a balloon in his mouth, tossed it gently in the air, and let it land harmlessly on the ground to show appropriate force levels.

Then Franklin selected another balloon and demonstrated proper targeting by gently tossing it toward an uncontested area of the battlefield, showing that competitive combat could be conducted without aggressive personal targeting.

"Franklin's providing technical training," Donald announced, though he was starting to realize that Franklin's referee role was expanding beyond anything he'd originally planned.

The participants were delighted by Franklin's demonstration and immediately began requesting additional coaching on water balloon throwing techniques, strategic positioning, and competitive ethics.

Franklin responded to these requests by conducting what could only be described as a comprehensive water balloon warfare training clinic. He demonstrated proper grip techniques (as much as was possible with a pig snout), showed optimal throwing trajectories, and provided tactical consultation on team coordination and battlefield positioning.

"This is better than the actual competition," Mary Flynn observed, watching Franklin explain defensive strategies through a combination of honking and physical demonstration.

Donald realized that Franklin had once again transformed his carefully planned business venture into something completely different and significantly more entertaining than originally intended. Instead of organizing competitive combat, Donald was now hosting what appeared to be a pig-led educational workshop on water balloon warfare techniques.

"Franklin's expanding the service offering," Donald told Eddie and Frankie during a brief operational break. "He's providing added value that we never advertised but that's clearly enhancing customer satisfaction."

The problem was that Franklin's expanded educational role was attracting attention beyond the paying participants. Kids from throughout the neighbourhood had heard about the pig who was teaching water balloon combat techniques, and they were arriving to observe Franklin's training clinic.

"Can we watch Franklin's demonstration?" asked a group of kids who hadn't paid admission fees.

Donald faced another challenging business decision. Allowing non-paying observers would undermine his admission fee structure, but turning away potential customers could damage neighbourhood relations and future marketing opportunities.

"Franklin's training clinic is included in premium admission," Donald announced. "But we're offering a special observer rate of twenty-five cents for non-participants who want to benefit from Franklin's educational services."

This compromise generated additional revenue while maintaining the value of full admission, and Donald felt pleased with his adaptive pricing strategy.

But Franklin's educational activities were becoming more ambitious by the minute. He'd moved beyond basic throwing technique instruction and was now providing what appeared to be comprehensive strategic consultation.

Franklin demonstrated flanking manoeuvres by trotting around imaginary opponents. He showed defensive positioning by creating barriers using empty water balloon containers. He even illustrated team coordination by honking signals that participants could use to communicate tactical information during combat.

"Franklin's conducting advanced military education," Brains Morrison observed. "This is like actual strategy training."

Donald watched Franklin lead twenty kids through sophisticated tactical exercises and realized that his pig was providing educational value that probably exceeded what most summer camps offered.

"Franklin's a natural teacher," Lisa said, approaching Donald while Franklin demonstrated the proper use of battlefield terrain for strategic advantage.

"Franklin understands that knowledge sharing enhances competitive quality for everyone," Donald replied, though he was still trying to understand how Franklin had developed such sophisticated military strategy knowledge.

The morning concluded with what Franklin apparently considered the logical culmination of his educational program: a demonstration battle where Franklin served as both strategic consultant and active participant.

Franklin organized the participants into two evenly matched teams and positioned himself as mobile tactical advisor, trotting between teams to provide real-time consultation on positioning, timing, and ammunition conservation.

The resulting battle was the most sophisticated water balloon combat Donald had ever seen. Participants used Franklin's strategic training to develop coordinated attacks, defensive formations, and tactical adaptations that would have impressed actual military planners.

More importantly, everyone was having tremendous fun. Franklin's training had elevated random water balloon throwing into genuine strategic competition, and participants were clearly engaged at a level that exceeded simple summer entertainment.

"This is the best water balloon fight ever," declared several participants simultaneously.

Donald felt the satisfaction that came from successful event management and educational service delivery. He'd provided structured entertainment, Franklin had delivered unexpected educational value, and participants were clearly receiving premium recreational experiences that justified their admission fees.

By noon, when the competition officially concluded, Donald had generated eleven dollars and seventy-five cents in admission fees, three dollars and forty cents in refreshment sales, and two dollars and ten cents in tips for Franklin's educational services.

After expenses (water balloons, refreshments, and battlefield maintenance supplies), Donald calculated a net profit of fourteen dollars and fifty cents, which split three ways meant nearly five dollars each.

"That's more money than I made in two weeks at my paper route," Eddie said as they counted the final receipts.

"That's more money than I've ever had at one time," Frankie added.

Donald felt the kind of confidence that came from genuine business success and educational service delivery. "This is just the beginning," he said. "Once word spreads about the quality of Franklin's strategic training programs, we'll have people requesting advanced military education workshops all summer long."

Franklin, exhausted from his dual role as referee and tactical instructor, honked agreement and settled down for a well-deserved nap.

As Donald cleaned up the battlefield and calculated plans for future warfare events, he felt confident that he'd found the perfect competitive response to the Feinberg twins' systematic approach.

Home delivery was efficient, but it couldn't compete with the kind of interactive educational entertainment that featured pig-led strategic training.

Of course, he didn't yet know that the Feinberg twins had spent the morning taking detailed notes on Franklin's tactical instruction methods, or that they were planning to incorporate "professional activity coordination" into their expanding service portfolio.

He also didn't know that Mrs. Henderson had spent Saturday morning on the phone with other neighbourhood parents, discussing "the escalating complexity of Trump family activities" and organizing what she was calling "concerned neighbour coordination."

But those were next week's challenges. Tonight, Donald had nearly five dollars in profit, a pig with proven military strategy abilities, and a summer full of educational warfare possibilities stretching ahead of him.

Franklin honked goodnight from his pen, and Donald fell asleep planning the advanced tactical training programs that would establish him as the neighbourhood's premier provider of strategic military education.

He still had no idea that the real war was about to begin.

The Delivery Service Debacle

The water balloon warfare championship had been such a tremendous success that by Tuesday morning, Donald was receiving business inquiries from parents throughout the neighbourhood. Mrs. Patterson had called to ask about "tactical training birthday parties." Mr. Kowalski wanted to know if Franklin offered "strategic consultation for family game nights." Even Mrs. Henderson, despite her ongoing concerns about pig-related property incidents, had grudgingly admitted that "the children seemed to learn something about teamwork."

But Donald's confidence in his military strategy business was shattered on Tuesday afternoon when he discovered the full scope of the Feinberg twins' competitive response.

It started when he noticed unusual bicycle traffic on Elm Street. Not just the normal Feinberg delivery riders, but an organized fleet of at least eight kids on bikes, all wearing matching blue t-shirts and following what appeared to be coordinated patrol routes throughout the neighbourhood.

"Eddie," Donald said, grabbing his friend's arm as they watched the bicycle brigade from the front porch. "Go find out what they're doing."

Eddie returned twenty minutes later with intelligence that made Donald's strategic planning significantly more complicated.

"They're not just doing delivery anymore," Eddie reported. "They've got mobile lemonade service, door-to-door snack sales, custom party planning, and something they're calling 'neighbourhood recreation coordination.'"

"Recreation coordination?" Donald felt his stomach drop.

"Madeline was telling Mrs. Chen that they provide 'comprehensive summer entertainment services with professional activity management and guaranteed customer satisfaction,'" Eddie continued. "They've got organized games, craft projects, reading clubs, and advanced group activities."

Donald stared at the Feinberg bicycle operation and realized that his competition wasn't just trying to steal his customers, they were systematically replicating and improving every business concept he'd developed.

"What about Franklin-style entertainment?" Donald asked desperately.

"They've got a dog," Eddie said quietly. "Golden retriever named Eisenhower. Apparently, he's been trained to perform tricks and coordinate group activities."

Donald felt the kind of strategic crisis that separated successful entrepreneurs from those who got outmanoeuvred by superior competition. The Feinbergs had studied his operational methods, identified his competitive advantages, and developed responses that matched or exceeded everything he'd accomplished.

"We need to accelerate our competitive timeline," Donald announced, pulling out his notebook to sketch emergency strategic planning. "If they're going to compete on organization and delivery, we'll compete on scale and innovation."

"What kind of scale?" Frankie asked nervously.

Donald looked at Franklin, who was listening to the conversation with obvious interest, and felt the kind of desperate inspiration that came in moments of genuine business crisis.

"Mobile operations," Donald said. "Instead of waiting for customers to come to us, we take the business directly to them. Door-to-door, real-time service delivery, and personalized customer experiences that no bicycle brigade can match."

The plan, as Donald explained it over the next hour, was elegantly ambitious. Instead of competing with the Feinbergs on their terms, he would create a mobile service operation that combined delivery convenience with Franklin's proven entertainment value.

"Franklin and I will conduct neighbourhood routes," Donald explained, sketching organizational diagrams. "We'll offer on-demand lemonade service, immediate party planning consultation, and Franklin's tactical training programs delivered directly to customers' homes."

"How are you going to carry lemonade around the neighbourhood?" Eddie asked.

"Portable beverage system," Donald replied. "I'll use my mother's picnic cooler, pre-mix the lemonade in thermoses, and provide fresh-served drinks anywhere in a six-block radius."

"And how is Franklin going to provide tactical training in people's backyards?"

Donald looked at Franklin, who was performing his sitting trick apparently just to demonstrate his readiness for expanded business responsibilities. "Franklin's educational programs are adaptable to any location. He's proven that he can provide strategic consultation, entertainment services, and crowd management regardless of venue."

This was mostly true, though Donald was beginning to realize that Franklin's approach to customer service often involved initiatives that exceeded planned operational parameters.

"What about the Feinbergs' bicycle advantage?" Frankie asked. "They can cover more territory faster than you can walking."

"Speed isn't everything," Donald replied, though he was privately concerned about the logistics of competing with an eight-bike delivery fleet. "We'll compete on service quality and customer experience. Personal attention and customized entertainment that you can't get from a bicycle brigade."

Wednesday was spent in intensive preparation for what Donald called "mobile service launch." He secured permission to borrow his mother's largest picnic cooler, developed portable lemonade recipes that would maintain quality during transportation, and created what he called "Franklin's mobile entertainment protocols."

The most challenging aspect was designing a system that would allow Franklin to participate in neighbourhood delivery routes while maintaining the safety and control standards his parents had established after previous business ventures.

"Franklin travels on a leash," Donald explained to his parents during Wednesday evening's operational briefing. "Professional pet management with complete supervision throughout the delivery route."

"A leash?" Mrs. Trump looked sceptical. "Donald, Franklin weighs sixty pounds and has his own opinions about where he wants to go. I'm not sure a leash is going to provide the control you think it will."

"Franklin's proven that he responds to professional management," Donald replied. "He understands business objectives and customer service priorities. A leash is just a formal communication tool."

This was optimistic reasoning, but Donald had purchased what the pet store assured him was a "heavy-duty livestock management system", essentially a very strong rope with clips on both ends that could theoretically provide guidance for ambitious pigs.

Fred Trump examined the leash with the expression of someone who'd learned to be cautious about his son's equipment purchases. "Donald, if Franklin gets loose during one of these delivery routes, you're both coming straight home and staying there."

"Franklin won't get loose," Donald promised. "This is a professional operation with complete safety protocols."

Thursday's test run confirmed that Franklin's leash training was going to require more strategic thinking than Donald had anticipated.

Franklin understood the concept of walking with Donald, but his interpretation of "delivery route" included systematic investigation of every interesting smell, sound, and visual curiosity within a three-block radius. What Donald had planned as efficient customer service delivery became a comprehensive neighbourhood exploration program guided by Franklin's natural curiosity.

"Franklin," Donald said as they paused for Franklin's seventh investigation of the morning, this time a fascinating scent trail near

Mrs. Patterson's garbage cans. "We need to maintain focus on customer service objectives."

Franklin honked acknowledgment but continued his thorough investigation of whatever had captured his attention.

By the time they'd completed one block of their planned delivery route, Donald realized that Franklin's participation was going to require significant adjustments to his efficiency projections. But he also noticed that Franklin's investigative approach was generating customer attention that no bicycle delivery could match.

"Is that your pig?" Mrs. Rodriguez called out from her front porch as Franklin conducted a detailed examination of her flower garden.

"This is Franklin Roosevelt, our mobile customer service coordinator," Donald replied, trying to turn Franklin's garden investigation into evidence of professional thoroughness. "He's conducting neighbourhood quality assessment as part of our comprehensive service delivery program."

Mrs. Rodriguez seemed amused by Franklin's systematic approach to flower sniffing. "What kind of service delivery?"

Donald seized the marketing opportunity. "Premium lemonade delivery, custom entertainment services, and tactical recreation planning. All provided directly to your location with personalized customer consultation."

"You mean I don't have to walk to your house to buy lemonade?"

"Completely mobile operation," Donald confirmed. "We bring the business to you."

Mrs. Rodriguez ordered two cups of classic lemonade, which Donald served from his portable beverage system while Franklin provided entertainment by performing his sitting trick and offering his hoof for formal introduction.

"That pig has better manners than most people," Mrs. Rodriguez observed, paying Donald thirty cents for the lemonade plus a ten-cent tip for Franklin's customer service.

Donald felt vindicated in his mobile strategy. Franklin's personal attention was clearly creating customer satisfaction that exceeded simple product delivery, and the tip structure suggested that people valued the enhanced service experience.

The morning's route took nearly three hours to complete, but Donald generated two dollars and sixty cents in revenue while establishing what he recognized as genuine customer relationships throughout the neighbourhood.

"This could work," Donald told Eddie and Frankie during Thursday afternoon's strategy session. "Franklin's mobile customer service creates personal connections that the Feinberg bicycle brigade can't match. We're competing on relationship quality rather than delivery speed."

Friday's expanded route testing confirmed both the potential and the complications of Franklin-based mobile service delivery.

Franklin had clearly grasped the concept of customer service calls and was eager to participate in neighbourhood business development. But his approach to professional service delivery included initiatives that Donald hadn't anticipated.

When they visited Mr. Chen's house to offer lemonade service, Franklin noticed that Mr. Chen's garden needed watering and began honking insistently until Donald agreed to help with plant irrigation.

"Franklin's providing value-added customer service," Donald explained as he operated Mr. Chen's garden hose while Franklin supervised water distribution. "He identifies customer needs that go beyond basic beverage delivery."

Mr. Chen was clearly impressed by Franklin's attention to his garden care needs. "That pig really knows about plants. Look how he's showing you exactly where the water should go."

Franklin was indeed providing detailed irrigation consultation, honking directions for optimal watering patterns and occasionally nudging Donald toward plants that appeared to need additional attention.

"Franklin has natural agricultural knowledge," Donald said, though he was beginning to realize that Franklin's customer service initiatives were expanding his delivery route timeline significantly.

What should have been a fifteen-minute lemonade delivery became a forty-five-minute garden care consultation, complete with Franklin's detailed assessment of Mr. Chen's vegetable growing strategies.

But Mr. Chen was so pleased with Franklin's horticultural expertise that he paid for three cups of lemonade, added a twenty-cent tip, and specifically requested that Donald and Franklin return the following week for additional garden consultation services.

"Franklin's creating recurring customer relationships," Donald told Eddie and Frankie during Friday afternoon's route analysis. "He's building the kind of service loyalty that generates long-term business sustainability."

The problem was that Franklin's approach to customer service was becoming increasingly comprehensive and time-consuming. By Friday afternoon, Donald's planned delivery route had expanded to include garden consultation, lawn care assessment, and what Franklin apparently considered essential pet care advice for neighbourhood dogs and cats.

"Franklin spent twenty minutes examining Mrs. Patterson's cat," Donald reported to his business partners. "Apparently he has opinions about proper feline nutrition and exercise requirements."

"Did Mrs. Patterson appreciate Franklin's pet care consultation?" Eddie asked.

"She bought four cups of lemonade and asked if Franklin could provide weekly wellness check services for Mr. Whiskers," Donald replied. "But it took us an hour and a half to complete what should have been a ten-minute delivery stop."

Donald was beginning to understand that Franklin's customer service approach was both his greatest competitive advantage and his most significant operational challenge. Franklin provided personal attention and value-added services that no bicycle delivery could match, but his comprehensive approach to customer needs made efficient route completion nearly impossible.

"We need to streamline Franklin's service delivery while maintaining his customer relationship advantages," Donald concluded. "Professional boundaries that preserve efficiency without compromising service quality."

Saturday's launch of the official mobile delivery service tested Donald's strategic planning against the reality of Franklin-based customer interaction.

Donald had prepared what he called "comprehensive mobile service protocols", planned routes, timing objectives, and service delivery standards that would allow them to compete effectively with the Feinberg bicycle operation.

Franklin had different ideas about customer service priorities.

Their first delivery call was to the Morrison house, where Brains's mother had requested lemonade service for a backyard barbecue. This should have been a straightforward commercial transaction, deliver beverages, collect payment, proceed to next customer.

But Franklin noticed that the Morrison barbecue included several young children who appeared to be having difficulty with organized game activities, and he apparently concluded that recreational consultation was part of comprehensive customer service.

Franklin began honking suggestions for improved game organization, demonstrated proper tag technique by gently chasing the children around the backyard, and provided what appeared to be strategic consultation for hide-and-seek activities.

"Franklin's providing recreational coordination services," Donald explained to Mrs. Morrison as her backyard barbecue transformed into a pig-led entertainment program.

"I've never seen children so engaged with organized activities," Mrs. Morrison replied, watching Franklin lead six kids through what appeared to be sophisticated tactical training exercises. "Where did you learn about child recreation management?"

"Franklin has natural educational instincts," Donald said, though he was privately amazed by Franklin's ability to adapt his military strategy knowledge to age-appropriate recreational activities.

The Morrison delivery call generated eight dollars in beverage sales, three dollars in tips for Franklin's entertainment services, and a request for weekly recreational consultation that could potentially become a significant recurring revenue stream.

But the call had also taken two and a half hours, which meant that Donald's planned six-stop delivery route was already behind schedule before they'd completed their first customer interaction.

"Franklin's service quality is generating customer satisfaction that exceeds our projections," Donald told Eddie and Frankie during a brief operational consultation while Franklin provided strategic advice to Mrs. Morrison's children about proper water balloon defensive positioning.

"But we're never going to complete our planned route at this pace," Eddie pointed out.

Donald realized that he faced a fundamental business decision: compete with the Feinbergs on delivery efficiency, or leverage Franklin's unique service capabilities to create a different kind of customer value.

"We pivot to premium service delivery," Donald announced. "Instead of trying to match bicycle speed, we offer comprehensive customer consultation that provides genuine value beyond simple product delivery."

This strategic adjustment proved prescient when they arrived at their second delivery call to find the Feinberg twins already there.

Mrs. Patterson had apparently ordered lemonade from both operations, either through confusion about scheduling or deliberate comparison shopping. When Donald and Franklin arrived at her front door, Madeline and Josephine were already in her backyard setting up what appeared to be a comprehensive recreational activity program.

"Donald," Mrs. Patterson said, opening the door with obvious concern. "I think there might have been some confusion about today's service delivery."

Donald looked past Mrs. Patterson to see the Feinberg operation in full deployment. They had two tables set up with professional efficiency, four kids in matching t-shirts providing activity coordination, and what appeared to be a systematic approach to entertainment delivery that made Donald's mobile service look decidedly amateur by comparison.

"No confusion," Donald replied, projecting confidence he didn't entirely feel. "We're here to provide our scheduled premium customer service consultation."

Franklin, apparently sensing competitive tension, honked authoritatively and performed his sitting trick to establish his professional credentials.

"Well," Mrs. Patterson said, "I suppose you could both provide services. The children would probably enjoy the variety."

This led to what Donald would later describe as "direct competitive market testing under controlled conditions" and what Eddie would remember as "the most awkward business situation ever."

Donald and Franklin found themselves providing mobile lemonade service and recreational consultation in the same backyard where the Feinberg twins were delivering their systematic activity coordination program. The two operations were forced to work in parallel while a dozen neighbourhood kids compared service quality in real time.

The contrast was immediately obvious. The Feinbergs had organization, efficiency, and professional presentation. Donald had Franklin.

Madeline and Josephine set up structured craft activities with pre-planned supply distribution and step-by-step instruction protocols. Franklin wandered among the children, providing personal attention and custom entertainment based on individual interest levels.

The twins coordinated group games with precise timing and rule enforcement. Franklin adapted activities spontaneously based on participant enthusiasm and attention spans.

The Feinbergs maintained professional distance while delivering consistent service quality. Franklin formed genuine personal relationships with each child while providing educational consultation that exceeded anyone's expectations.

"This is fascinating," Mrs. Patterson observed to Donald during a brief operational break. "Two completely different approaches to children's entertainment. Very educational."

Donald realized that Mrs. Patterson was essentially conducting a live comparison test of competing business models, and he wasn't entirely sure which approach was winning.

The Feinberg operation was undeniably impressive. Their activity coordination was smooth, their supply management was efficient, and their customer interaction was professionally consistent. Children completed craft projects successfully, participated in games with clear rules and fair outcomes, and received exactly the level of supervised entertainment that parents expected from premium service providers.

But Franklin was creating something completely different. Instead of structured activities, he was providing personalized attention that adapted to each child's interests and personality. Instead of following predetermined programming, he was responding to genuine moments of curiosity, creativity, and individual expression.

"Franklin's really listening to what the kids want," Lisa Chen observed. She'd arrived to help with her younger cousin's participation in the backyard activities and was clearly comparing the two entertainment approaches.

Donald watched Franklin conduct what appeared to be individual consultation sessions with different children, helping one kid with strategic planning for a complex building project, providing encouragement to another who was struggling with craft coordination, offering gentle tactical advice to a third who was having difficulty with group game participation.

"Franklin understands that different customers have different service needs," Donald said, trying to articulate Franklin's approach in business terms. "He provides customized consultation rather than standardized programming."

"It's like he actually cares about each kid individually," Lisa replied.

Donald felt a moment of recognition. Franklin wasn't just providing customer service, he was forming genuine relationships. The pig seemed to understand something about individual attention and personal connection that Donald was still learning about business and life.

The competitive comparison continued for two hours, with both operations providing parallel entertainment services while the children moved freely between structured Feinberg activities and Franklin's personalized consultation sessions.

"Kids like both approaches," Mrs. Patterson told Donald as the afternoon wound down. "The twins provide excellent organization, and Franklin provides something I can't quite describe. Personal attention, maybe. Individual connection."

Donald tallied the afternoon's results and realized that while the Feinbergs had served more customers and completed more activities, Franklin had generated more tips, more requests for return visits, and more genuine enthusiasm from participants.

"Different business models," Donald concluded. "They're competing on efficiency and scale. We're competing on relationship quality and personalized service."

But Donald also realized that the direct competitive comparison had revealed something important about the neighbourhood market. There was clearly demand for both approaches, systematic organization and personal attention, and customers seemed to value different service qualities depending on their specific needs and preferences.

"Maybe the market's big enough for multiple service providers," Eddie suggested during Saturday morning's strategy session.

"Or maybe we need to differentiate our service offering more clearly," Donald replied. "Establish market positioning that leverages

Franklin's unique capabilities while avoiding direct competition with the Feinbergs' operational strengths."

Donald spent Saturday morning developing what he called "strategic market differentiation analysis." Instead of trying to match the twins' delivery efficiency, he would focus on developing Franklin's educational and consultation services into a specialized business offering that couldn't be replicated by bicycle operations.

"Franklin's Strategic Consultation Services," Donald announced to his business partners. "Custom tactical training, personalized recreational planning, and individual attention for customers who want more than standardized programming."

"That sounds professional," Frankie said.

"That sounds expensive," Eddie added.

"Premium services command premium pricing," Donald replied. "Customers who appreciate Franklin's personalized approach will pay for quality consultation that they can't get anywhere else."

Saturday afternoon's test of the new service model proved that Donald's strategic differentiation was both viable and profitable.

Their first consultation call was with the Kowalski family, where Franklin provided what Donald called "comprehensive recreational assessment and strategic planning services." This involved Franklin observing the twins' play patterns, identifying their individual interests and skill levels, and developing customized activity recommendations that matched their specific entertainment preferences.

Franklin spent forty-five minutes with each twin, providing personalized attention that resulted in detailed recreational plans, improved coordination between the brothers, and what their mother described as "the most constructive play session they've had all summer."

"Franklin really understands children," Mrs. Kowalski told Donald as she paid five dollars for the consultation services, more than Donald had ever charged for a single customer interaction.

"Franklin's educational background includes child development and recreational psychology," Donald replied, though he had no idea where Franklin had acquired his obvious expertise in individual consultation.

The second consultation call was even more successful. Mr. and Mrs. Rodriguez had requested assistance with planning their daughter's birthday party, specifically asking for "the kind of personal attention that Franklin provides."

Franklin spent two hours conducting what appeared to be comprehensive party planning consultation. He assessed the available space, evaluated potential entertainment options, provided tactical advice for game organization, and even offered suggestions for food service positioning that would optimize guest flow and minimize cleanup requirements.

"That pig knows more about party planning than most adults," Mr. Rodriguez observed, watching Franklin demonstrate optimal table placement through a combination of honking and physical positioning.

Donald felt vindicated in his strategic differentiation approach. Franklin's consultation services were generating premium pricing, customer satisfaction that exceeded expectations, and requests for ongoing professional relationship that could provide sustainable revenue throughout the summer.

But Franklin's consultation success was also attracting attention that Donald hadn't anticipated.

By Saturday evening, word of Franklin's personalized consultation services had spread beyond Donald's immediate customer base. Parents throughout the neighbourhood were calling to inquire about Franklin's availability for individual problem-solving sessions, educational consultation, and what Mrs. Chen described as "that special kind of attention Franklin provides to children who need extra support."

"Franklin's developing a professional reputation independent of our business operation," Donald told his parents during Saturday dinner. "People are specifically requesting his consultation services."

"What kind of consultation services?" Mrs. Trump asked.

"Child development support, recreational planning, educational assistance," Donald replied. "Franklin has natural abilities in individual attention and problem-solving that parents really appreciate."

Donald was trying to present Franklin's expanding consultation practice as evidence of successful business development, but he was privately beginning to realize that Franklin's professional capabilities were exceeding his own strategic planning abilities.

"Donald," his father said carefully, "it sounds like Franklin is developing his own business relationships. What's your role in these consultation services?"

This was exactly the question Donald had been hoping to avoid. Franklin's consultation success was clearly based on the pig's natural abilities rather than Donald's business management, and customers were increasingly interested in Franklin's services rather than Donald's organizational coordination.

"I provide operational support and customer interface management," Donald said. "Franklin handles the technical consultation, and I manage the business logistics."

This was diplomatically accurate, though Donald was beginning to suspect that Franklin could probably handle customer interface management as well if he needed to.

Sunday morning brought a development that changed Donald's understanding of his competitive position entirely.

Mrs. Chen called to request Franklin's consultation services for Lisa's upcoming birthday party, but she had a specific request that surprised Donald.

"Would it be possible," Mrs. Chen asked, "for Franklin to provide consultation services without the business operation aspects? Lisa was hoping Franklin could just come over as a friend rather than as a professional service provider."

Donald felt his carefully constructed business model shifting underneath him. "You want Franklin to visit without charging consultation fees?"

"Lisa has become quite fond of Franklin," Mrs. Chen explained. "She was hoping they could just spend some time together without the formal business structure. Maybe Franklin could help her plan the party as a friend rather than as a hired consultant."

Donald looked at Franklin, who was listening to the phone conversation with obvious interest, and realized that his pig had apparently developed personal relationships that transcended commercial transactions.

"Franklin makes his own social decisions," Donald said finally. "If he wants to visit Lisa as a friend, that's between them."

What happened next demonstrated that Franklin's understanding of business and friendship was considerably more sophisticated than Donald had realized.

Franklin trotted over to the phone and honked twice, which Donald had learned was Franklin's signal for enthusiastic agreement.

Then Franklin performed his sitting trick and looked expectantly at Donald, clearly communicating that he wanted to accept Lisa's invitation.

"Franklin would be delighted to provide friendly party planning assistance," Donald told Mrs. Chen. "No commercial fees required."

Sunday afternoon's visit to the Chen house revealed the depth of Franklin's social intelligence and Donald's own learning curve about the difference between business relationships and genuine friendships.

Franklin approached Lisa's party planning with the same systematic attention he'd applied to commercial consultation, but without the formal structure that Donald had imposed on his professional services. Instead of providing strategic recommendations through Donald's business interface, Franklin communicated directly with Lisa about her party preferences and ideas.

Donald found himself observing rather than managing as Franklin and Lisa developed party plans through a combination of Franklin's honking, Lisa's creative suggestions, and what appeared to be genuine collaborative problem-solving.

"Franklin really understands what I want," Lisa told Donald as Franklin provided tactical advice for optimal party game organization. "It's like he knows exactly what would be fun without me having to explain everything."

Donald watched Franklin adapt his consultation approach to Lisa's individual personality and interests, and realized that Franklin's greatest ability wasn't strategic planning or customer service, it was authentic connection with people who appreciated his genuine attention and care.

"Franklin's not just a business partner," Donald said slowly, understanding something important for the first time. "He's actually a friend."

Franklin honked agreement and performed his sitting trick for Lisa, who laughed and scratched behind his ears with obvious affection.

As Donald walked home with Franklin that evening, he felt the kind of strategic clarity that came from understanding the difference between commercial success and personal relationships.

The Feinberg twins were excellent at business efficiency and organizational delivery. But Franklin was building something that couldn't be replicated by any bicycle brigade or systematic service protocol, genuine connections with people who valued authentic attention and individual care.

"Franklin," Donald said as they approached home, "I think we might be in the wrong business."

Franklin honked thoughtfully and looked at Donald with what appeared to be understanding.

"Maybe instead of trying to compete with the Feinbergs on their terms," Donald continued, "we should focus on what you do best. Real relationships. Genuine service. Personal attention that actually helps people."

Franklin performed his sitting trick and honked what sounded like enthusiastic agreement.

As Donald settled Franklin in his pen for the night, he felt confident that he'd identified the strategic direction that would make their partnership genuinely successful. Not just profitable, but meaningful.

Of course, he didn't yet know that the Feinberg twins had spent Sunday afternoon developing their own "personalized service enhancement protocols," or that Mrs. Henderson's "concerned neighbour coordination" was planning its first formal intervention for the following week.

But those were tomorrow's challenges. Tonight, Donald had discovered that his pig was capable of genuine friendship, and that friendship might be more valuable than any business competitive advantage.

Franklin honked goodnight, and Donald fell asleep planning consultation services that would focus on authentic connection rather than commercial efficiency.

He still had no idea that the real test of friendship was about to begin.

Independence Day Spectacular

The Fourth of July was supposed to be Donald Trump's greatest triumph. After weeks of escalating competition with the Feinberg twins, mounting neighbourhood tensions, and Franklin's increasingly independent approach to customer service, Donald had conceived what he considered the ultimate business strategy: a patriotic extravaganza that would demonstrate once and for all the superiority of Trump-Franklin partnership over systematic bicycle efficiency.

The plan was ambitious even by Donald's standards. Instead of simply participating in the neighbourhood's traditional Independence Day block party, Donald would create a parallel celebration that featured premium entertainment, exclusive activities, and Franklin's proven consultation services, all organized with the kind of professional presentation that would establish permanent market dominance.

"It's not just a party," Donald explained to Eddie and Frankie during Monday's planning session, three days before the holiday. "It's a comprehensive patriotic experience. Food service, entertainment coordination, educational programming, and recreational activities that demonstrate real American entrepreneurial values."

Franklin, listening from his pen with obvious interest, honked what Donald interpreted as patriotic enthusiasm.

"What kind of educational programming?" Eddie asked, though his tone suggested he was already anticipating complications.

"Franklin's Tactical Independence Training," Donald replied, consulting his notebook where he'd been sketching increasingly elaborate organizational diagrams. "Strategic games that teach American historical values, competitive activities that demonstrate democratic principles, and group coordination exercises that build community spirit."

"Donald," Frankie said carefully, "the neighbourhood already has a Fourth of July block party. With games and food and everything. Why do we need a separate celebration?"

Donald had anticipated this question, and he'd developed what he considered a compelling strategic rationale.

"The traditional block party is fine for people who want ordinary neighbourhood entertainment," Donald said. "But we're offering premium patriotic experiences for families who appreciate professional organization and unique educational value. Market differentiation through superior service quality."

This sounded reasonable in business theory, but Eddie was beginning to recognize the pattern of Donald's escalating ambitions.

"Donald, creating a competing Fourth of July celebration might not be the best way to improve neighbourhood relations," Eddie pointed out. "Especially after Mrs. Henderson's been talking to other parents about 'Trump family activity management.'"

Donald had been trying to ignore Mrs. Henderson's "concerned neighbour coordination," but he was aware that several parents had been discussing what they called "appropriate supervision standards" and "reasonable entertainment boundaries" in conversations that seemed to focus specifically on his business ventures.

"Mrs. Henderson doesn't understand entrepreneurial innovation," Donald replied. "Once she sees the quality of our patriotic programming, she'll appreciate the educational value we're providing to the community."

Franklin honked from his pen, though whether this indicated agreement or concern was difficult to determine.

Tuesday's preparation involved what Donald called "comprehensive patriotic supply procurement and venue optimization." This mostly meant purchasing red, white, and blue streamers from the five-and-dime, borrowing additional tables from neighbours who were willing to support educational programming, and creating what Donald considered sophisticated decorative presentations.

More challenging was developing Franklin's role in patriotic entertainment. Donald had envisioned Franklin providing tactical training with a specifically American historical focus, but translating Franklin's proven military strategy abilities into educational programming required more creativity than Donald had initially anticipated.

"Franklin will demonstrate Revolutionary War tactical principles," Donald explained to his parents during Tuesday evening's operational briefing. "Strategic positioning, resource management, and coordinated group activities that teach historical lessons while providing entertainment value."

"Revolutionary War tactics?" Mrs. Trump looked sceptical. "Donald, Franklin's a pig, not a history professor."

"Franklin has natural strategic abilities that can be adapted to historical education," Donald replied. "He understands group dynamics, tactical positioning, and resource allocation. Those are the same principles that won American independence."

This was creative interpretation of Franklin's abilities, but Donald was convinced that Franklin's strategic intelligence could be channelled into genuinely educational programming.

Fred Trump examined Donald's planning materials with the expression of someone who'd learned to be cautious about his son's ambitious projects. "Donald, what exactly are you planning to do differently from the regular block party?"

"Enhanced programming," Donald said. "Professional organization, educational activities, and premium service delivery that demonstrates superior event management capabilities."

"Son," his father said slowly, "it sounds like you're trying to compete with the entire neighbourhood's Fourth of July celebration. That's not entrepreneurship, that's picking a fight with everyone we live near."

Donald felt his first serious doubt about his patriotic strategy. But he'd already committed to the expanded programming, sent invitations throughout the neighbourhood, and promised participants the most tremendous Independence Day experience they'd ever seen.

"This is about providing choices," Donald said. "Families can participate in traditional block party activities, or they can experience our premium patriotic programming. Market diversity benefits everyone."

Wednesday's final preparations included what Donald called "tactical educational material development" and what Franklin apparently considered intensive professional training for his expanded historical consultation role.

Donald had borrowed history books from the library and spent Tuesday night reading about Revolutionary War strategy, specifically looking for tactical principles that Franklin could demonstrate through his proven ability to coordinate group activities and provide strategic consultation.

"Franklin," Donald explained during Wednesday morning's training session, "tomorrow you'll be providing historical education along with your regular entertainment services. Revolutionary War tactics, strategic principles that founded American independence, and group coordination exercises that teach democratic values."

Franklin honked acknowledgment and performed his sitting trick, though Donald suspected that Franklin's understanding of American historical principles was probably more intuitive than academic.

The training session involved Donald reading historical descriptions of Revolutionary War battles while Franklin provided what appeared to be tactical commentary through strategic honking and physical positioning. By Wednesday afternoon, Donald was convinced that Franklin had grasped the essential principles of 18th-century military strategy.

"Franklin understands that American independence was won through superior tactical thinking and coordinated group action," Donald told Eddie and Frankie during Wednesday evening's final planning review. "Tomorrow he'll demonstrate those same principles through interactive educational programming."

Thursday morning dawned clear and hot, perfect Independence Day weather. Donald spent the early hours completing venue preparation and reviewing his operational protocols. By nine o'clock, everything was ready for what he expected would be the most successful patriotic celebration in neighbourhood history.

The Trump backyard had been transformed into what Donald called "comprehensive patriotic entertainment venue." Red, white, and blue streamers decorated the fence and tables. American flags marked strategic activity stations. A large banner reading "FRANKLIN'S INDEPENDENCE DAY SPECTACULAR - PROFESSIONAL PATRIOTIC PROGRAMMING" stretched between two maple trees.

Franklin had been positioned at the centre of the venue, wearing a red, white, and blue ribbon around his neck that Donald had designed to indicate his role as historical education coordinator.

"Today," Donald announced to Franklin during the final pre-event briefing, "we demonstrate that American entrepreneurial values and superior service quality can compete with any systematic operational approach."

Franklin honked officially and performed his sitting trick, establishing his readiness for expanded educational responsibilities.

The first participants arrived at ten o'clock, Tommy Kowalski and his brother, followed by several kids from Donald's school and a few families who'd specifically requested Franklin's historical education services.

"Welcome to Franklin's Independence Day Spectacular!" Donald announced as each participant arrived. "Today's programming features Revolutionary War tactical training, democratic principle demonstrations, and patriotic group activities coordinated by Franklin Roosevelt, the neighbourhood's leading strategic education specialist!"

The early arrivals paid their admission fees (Donald had established premium patriotic pricing at seventy-five cents per participant) and gathered around Franklin for the opening educational presentation.

"Franklin will now demonstrate the tactical principles that won American independence," Donald announced, though he realized he wasn't entirely sure how Franklin planned to provide historical education.

Franklin approached this challenge with his characteristic systematic intelligence. He began by dividing the assembled participants into two groups, what Donald quickly designated as "Colonial forces" and "British forces", and then provided what appeared to be strategic consultation to both sides about proper Revolutionary War tactical positioning.

Using honking signals and physical demonstration, Franklin showed the Colonial forces how to use terrain advantages, coordinate group movements, and maintain communication during strategic operations. Then he provided similar consultation to the British forces about systematic advance techniques, supply line management, and organized retreat procedures.

"Franklin's providing balanced historical education," Donald announced, though he was privately amazed by Franklin's apparent understanding of 18th century military strategy. "He's demonstrating that American victory required understanding both Colonial innovation and British systematic approaches."

The participants were clearly engaged by Franklin's interactive historical programming. Instead of listening to boring lectures about Revolutionary War battles, they were receiving hands-on tactical training that made historical principles immediately relevant and entertaining.

"This is way better than school history class," declared Brains Morrison, who was leading the Colonial forces with strategic thinking that would have impressed actual Revolutionary War generals.

Franklin's historical education program continued for an hour, with increasingly sophisticated demonstrations of tactical principles, democratic decision-making processes, and group coordination techniques that translated abstract historical concepts into concrete interactive experiences.

"Franklin really understands history," Lisa Chen observed. She'd arrived with several friends to participate in the patriotic programming and was clearly impressed by Franklin's educational approach.

"Franklin has natural historical intelligence," Donald replied, though he was beginning to wonder where Franklin had acquired his obvious expertise in Revolutionary War strategy and democratic principles.

The morning's success was interrupted at eleven-thirty by the arrival of an unexpected competitor: the regular neighbourhood Fourth of July block party.

Donald had assumed that his premium patriotic programming would coexist peacefully with the traditional celebration, but he'd underestimated the organizational capabilities of neighbourhood adults who'd been planning their annual Independence Day festivities for months.

The block party setup began two houses down from the Trump property and rapidly expanded to include professional-quality food service, organized entertainment, and what appeared to be significantly more comprehensive programming than Donald had anticipated.

"They've got a barbecue grill, organized games, and live music," Eddie reported after conducting reconnaissance of the competing celebration.

"Plus, ice cream, patriotic crafts, and what looks like actual historical reenactment activities," Frankie added.

Donald looked at his own operation, which suddenly seemed considerably less impressive by comparison, and felt the familiar strategic panic that came when superior competition appeared without warning.

"We need to escalate our programming immediately," Donald announced. "If they're going to compete on scale and traditional activities, we'll compete on innovation and educational value."

"How do we escalate?" Eddie asked.

Donald looked at Franklin, who was listening to the conversation with obvious concern, and felt the kind of desperate inspiration that came in moments of genuine crisis.

"Revolutionary War reenactment," Donald announced. "Franklin leads historically accurate tactical demonstrations while we provide immersive educational experiences that put participants directly into American historical events."

"Revolutionary War reenactment?" Frankie repeated. "Donald, we don't have costumes or weapons or anything that looks like historical reenactment."

"We have Franklin," Donald replied. "And Franklin has proven strategic abilities that can provide authentic tactical education. We'll create experiential history programming that makes the past come alive through interactive participation."

Donald's reenactment concept involved Franklin leading the assembled participants through what Donald called "authentic Revolutionary War strategic scenarios." Using water balloons as ammunition and the backyard as battlefield terrain, Franklin would coordinate historically accurate tactical exercises that would provide both education and entertainment.

"Franklin will serve as both historical consultant and commanding officer," Donald explained to the growing crowd of participants. "You'll experience real Revolutionary War strategic challenges while learning about the tactical intelligence that won American independence."

Franklin honked officially and began organizing the participants into what appeared to be historically appropriate military units.

The problem was that Franklin's approach to Revolutionary War reenactment included tactical innovations that probably hadn't been available to 18th-century armies.

Franklin began by conducting advanced reconnaissance of the battlefield terrain, identifying strategic positions, defensive advantages, and supply line vulnerabilities with systematic thoroughness that exceeded what Donald had expected from historical education programming.

Then Franklin organized the participants into coordinated tactical units with communication systems, specialized roles, and strategic objectives that reflected genuinely sophisticated military planning.

"Franklin's providing graduate-level military education," Brains Morrison observed, watching Franklin demonstrate flanking manoeuvres that incorporated advanced group coordination techniques.

Donald felt proud of Franklin's educational capabilities, but he was also beginning to realize that Franklin's reenactment programming was becoming more complex and realistic than he'd intended for neighbourhood entertainment.

The situation escalated when Franklin decided that authentic Revolutionary War experience required actual competitive engagement between opposing forces.

Instead of conducting educational demonstrations with cooperative participants, Franklin organized what appeared to be genuine tactical combat between Colonial and British forces, complete with strategic objectives, victory conditions, and what Donald recognized as seriously competitive engagement.

The resulting battle was the most sophisticated military exercise Donald had ever seen conducted by neighbourhood children. Franklin coordinated both sides with tactical signals, provided real-time strategic consultation, and maintained battlefield awareness that would have impressed professional military observers.

But Franklin's reenactment was also generating noise levels, competitive intensity, and participant enthusiasm that was attracting attention from the competing block party celebration.

"What's happening over there?" Donald could hear parents asking from the direction of the traditional festivities.

"Sounds like some kind of war game," someone replied.

"Is that the Trump boy with his pig again?"

Donald realized that Franklin's historical education programming was creating exactly the kind of neighbourhood attention that his parents had warned him to avoid.

"Franklin," Donald called out during a brief tactical pause, "maybe we should reduce the volume levels of our educational programming?"

But Franklin was clearly enjoying his role as Revolutionary War commanding officer, and the participants were having too much fun with authentic tactical combat to support any reduction in competitive intensity.

The crisis peaked when Franklin decided that genuine Revolutionary War experience required coordinated assault on enemy strategic positions, which, in Franklin's tactical assessment, included the traditional block party's food service area.

Franklin organized a flanking manoeuvre that involved sending Colonial forces around the edge of the Trump property to conduct reconnaissance of the block party's organizational structure. This was supposed to be educational observation, but Franklin's military training had been thorough, and the participants approached their reconnaissance mission with genuine tactical seriousness.

"We're just observing enemy supply lines," Tommy Kowalski announced as he led a squad of Colonial forces toward the block party barbecue area.

"For historical education purposes," added Mary Flynn, who was providing strategic coordination for what appeared to be a genuinely planned military operation.

Donald watched his Revolutionary War reenactment participants disappear into the crowd of the traditional block party and realized that Franklin's educational programming had just evolved into actual neighbourhood invasion.

"Franklin!" Donald called out in alarm. "Strategic recall! Bring everyone back to base camp!"

But Franklin had apparently concluded that the reconnaissance mission was proceeding according to proper military protocols, and he was providing tactical support by coordinating reserve forces for potential follow-up operations.

Franklin organized the remaining participants into what appeared to be backup tactical units while maintaining strategic communication with the reconnaissance forces who'd infiltrated the block party.

"Franklin's conducting advanced military operations," Brains Morrison observed with obvious admiration. "This is like actual war planning."

Donald felt a moment of pure panic. Franklin's Revolutionary War education had become so realistic that Donald was essentially coordinating a neighbourhood military campaign against the traditional Fourth of July celebration.

"This is historical reenactment!" Donald called out to anyone who might be listening. "Educational programming with authentic tactical elements!"

But Franklin's educational approach was becoming increasingly difficult to distinguish from actual military operations, and the participants were clearly engaged at a level that exceeded simple summer entertainment.

The situation reached crisis level when Franklin decided that effective Revolutionary War strategy required securing enemy supply assets.

The reconnaissance forces had reported back that the block party featured extensive food service operations with inadequate defensive positioning. Franklin apparently concluded that Colonial forces should demonstrate proper tactical resource acquisition through coordinated supply line interdiction.

This meant that Franklin led a coordinated assault on the block party's food service area, with participants using water balloons as ammunition and Franklin providing strategic coordination for what appeared to be genuine military engagement.

"WHAT ARE THOSE CHILDREN DOING?" Donald heard Mrs. Henderson's voice rising above the general commotion.

"Revolutionary War reenactment!" Donald called back, though he was beginning to realize that Franklin's interpretation of historical education had exceeded what most adults would consider appropriate neighbourhood programming.

"GET THAT PIG AWAY FROM THE POTATO SALAD!"

Donald looked toward the block party to see Franklin coordinating what could only be described as a full-scale tactical assault on the food service area. Participants were using advanced water balloon techniques to create diversions while Franklin directed strategic positioning for optimal supply line disruption.

"Franklin!" Donald called out desperately. "Cease-fire! Educational programming concluded!"

But Franklin had clearly committed to the authenticity of his Revolutionary War reenactment, and he was providing military leadership that exceeded anything the actual Continental Army had probably achieved.

Franklin's tactical coordination was so effective that within minutes, the Colonial forces had successfully captured the block party's entire dessert table, established defensive positions around the barbecue grill, and were conducting what appeared to be organized negotiation for prisoner exchange with the adult supervisors.

"Donald Trump!" Mrs. Henderson's voice carried clearly across the battlefield. "Get over here right now!"

Donald approached the captured food service area with as much dignity as he could manage while Franklin continued providing tactical consultation to participants who were clearly having the time of their lives with authentic Revolutionary War strategic engagement.

"Mrs. Henderson," Donald said, projecting professional calm despite the chaos surrounding him, "this is educational programming that demonstrates American historical values through interactive participation."

"This is a pig, leading children in an attack on our neighbourhood barbecue!" Mrs. Henderson replied.

"Revolutionary War reenactment," Donald corrected. "Franklin's providing historical education that makes Colonial tactical principles immediately relevant and engaging."

Mrs. Henderson looked at Franklin, who was currently coordinating supply line management while participants organized the captured desserts according to strategic value and nutritional content.

"That pig has taken over our entire food service operation," Mrs. Henderson observed.

"Franklin's demonstrating proper military resource acquisition," Donald replied, though he was beginning to realize that Franklin's educational approach might have exceeded appropriate boundaries for neighbourhood entertainment.

The situation required immediate diplomatic intervention, but Donald discovered that Franklin had established such effective tactical control that negotiating the return of captured food service assets was going to require genuine strategic planning.

"Franklin," Donald said, approaching his pig with the respect due to a successful military commander, "perhaps we should transition from active tactical engagement to victory celebration protocols?"

Franklin looked at Donald and honked what sounded like strategic assessment. Then he performed his sitting trick and began coordinating what appeared to be organized withdrawal from the captured food service positions.

Under Franklin's direction, the participants carefully returned all captured desserts, cleaned up any tactical disruption damage, and organized themselves into formation for what Franklin apparently considered appropriate post-engagement military discipline.

"Franklin's conducting professional military conclusion procedures," Donald announced to the assembled crowd of block party participants and concerned parents.

"Franklin's the best general ever," declared Tommy Kowalski, standing at attention while Franklin conducted what appeared to be formal tactical review procedures.

Donald realized that Franklin's Revolutionary War educational programming had been genuinely successful, the participants had learned about Colonial tactical principles, experienced authentic strategic coordination, and clearly understood the military intelligence that had won American independence.

The problem was that Franklin's educational effectiveness had also demonstrated to every parent in the neighbourhood that Donald's business ventures were becoming increasingly complex and potentially disruptive to community peace.

"Donald," Mrs. Chen approached him while Franklin completed his post-engagement inspection procedures. "That was... quite an educational experience."

"Franklin provides comprehensive historical programming," Donald replied, though he was trying to assess whether Mrs. Chen's tone indicated approval or concern.

"Lisa learned more about Revolutionary War strategy in two hours than she has in two years of school history classes," Mrs. Chen continued. "Franklin's obviously very knowledgeable about military principles."

Donald felt cautiously optimistic that Franklin's educational value was being recognized despite the tactical complications.

"However," Mrs. Chen added, "several parents are concerned about the intensity level of Franklin's programming. It's very effective education, but it might be more advanced than some families are comfortable with for neighbourhood summer activities."

Donald looked around the aftermath of Franklin's Revolutionary War reenactment and realized that while the educational programming had been tremendously successful, it had also generated exactly the kind of community attention that his parents had warned him to avoid.

Franklin, apparently sensing that post-engagement assessment was required, trotted over to Donald and honked what sounded like a request for strategic consultation.

"Franklin wants to know how we did," Donald translated.

"Franklin did excellent work," Mrs. Chen replied. "But maybe next time we could focus on Franklin's consultation abilities without the full military campaign aspects?"

Donald felt the kind of strategic clarity that came from understanding customer feedback and market positioning requirements.

"Franklin," he said, sitting down next to his pig while the neighbourhood adults continued discussing appropriate programming boundaries, "I think we might need to adjust our business model again."

Franklin honked thoughtfully and performed his sitting trick.

"You're really good at helping people and teaching things they want to learn," Donald continued. "But maybe we should focus on that instead of trying to create the biggest and most complicated programs possible."

Franklin looked at Donald with what appeared to be understanding and approval.

"Maybe the best business strategy isn't always trying to beat the competition," Donald said, realizing something important about genuine success. "Maybe sometimes it's just about doing what you're actually good at and helping people in ways they actually appreciate."

Franklin honked agreement and gently nudged Donald's hand with his snout.

As the neighbourhood adults organized cleanup and discussed what Donald heard described as "appropriate activity supervision guidelines," Donald felt the kind of learning that came from understanding the difference between ambitious planning and sustainable success.

The Fourth of July celebration continued peacefully for the rest of the afternoon, with Franklin providing individual consultation services to children who requested strategic advice, educational support, or simply personal attention from someone who listened carefully and responded thoughtfully.

"Franklin's really special," Lisa told Donald as the day wound down and families began heading home. "He pays attention to people in a way that makes them feel important."

Donald watched Franklin provide gentle encouragement to a younger child who'd been struggling with craft activities, and realized that Franklin's greatest ability wasn't strategic planning or competitive advantage, it was authentic care for people who needed support and attention.

"Franklin's taught me a lot about business," Donald said. "But I think he's teaching me more about friendship."

As Donald settled Franklin in his pen that evening, he felt confident that he'd learned something valuable about the difference between competing to win and working to help.

Of course, he didn't yet know that Mrs. Henderson's "concerned neighbour coordination" had reached a decision about "appropriate intervention strategies," or that the Feinberg twins had spent the afternoon developing their own "community service enhancement protocols" that would challenge Donald's customer relationships in ways he hadn't anticipated.

But those were tomorrow's challenges. Tonight, Donald had discovered that his pig was capable of genuine education and authentic friendship, and that those qualities might be more valuable than any competitive business advantage.

Franklin honked goodnight, and Donald fell asleep planning consultation services that would focus on helping people rather than beating competition.

He still had no idea that the real test of authentic friendship was about to begin.

The Rehabilitation Campaign

The Monday morning after Independence Day found Donald Trump in the most humbling position of his fifteen-year-old life: sitting on his front porch steps, wearing his regular clothes instead of his father's suit, watching the Feinberg twins conduct business in what used to be his neighbourhood territory.

The Fourth of July Revolutionary War incident had resulted in what his parents called "a serious reconsideration of summer business privileges" and what the neighbourhood parents had diplomatically termed "a temporary pause in Trump family organized activities." Donald was grounded from entrepreneurial ventures, Franklin was restricted to supervised backyard time only, and their combined reputation had shifted from "ambitious local entertainment" to "potential community disruption."

"The twins have six kids working for them now," Eddie reported, returning from reconnaissance of the Feinberg operation three blocks away. "Professional uniforms, expanded delivery routes, and something they're calling 'community service coordination.'"

Donald watched a steady stream of bicycle delivery riders heading in and out of Elm Street and felt the kind of strategic defeat that he'd only read about in his father's business magazines.

"What's community service coordination?" Donald asked, though he suspected the answer would make his current situation even more depressing.

"They're organizing neighbourhood improvement projects," Eddie explained. "Garden cleanup, elderly assistance, pet care services, and recreational programming for younger kids. All provided free of charge as 'community investment initiatives.'"

Donald felt his stomach drop. The Feinbergs hadn't just out-competed his business ventures, they'd elevated their approach to genuine community service that made Donald's profit-focused enterprises look selfish by comparison.

"They're not even charging money?" Frankie asked.

"That's the genius part," Eddie continued. "They're building community relationships and customer loyalty through free services. People feel good about supporting their business because they're giving back to the neighbourhood."

Donald stared at the Feinberg operation and realized that his competition had solved the fundamental strategic challenge that had been troubling him all summer: how to build genuine customer relationships while maintaining sustainable business success.

"They're playing a completely different game," Donald said slowly. "Not just better business, better community citizenship."

From his pen in the backyard, Franklin honked what sounded like thoughtful agreement.

"Franklin wants to know what our strategic response is going to be," Frankie translated.

Donald looked at Franklin, who was listening to the conversation with obvious interest despite being confined to supervised backyard activities. Since the Fourth of July incident, Franklin had been noticeably quieter, spending more time observing neighbourhood activities and less time planning what Donald had learned to recognize as independent initiatives.

"I don't think we have a strategic response," Donald admitted. "I think we might need to completely rethink what we're trying to accomplish."

This was the first time all summer that Donald had acknowledged fundamental strategic uncertainty, and Eddie and Frankie exchanged glances that suggested they'd been expecting this moment for weeks.

"What do you mean, rethink?" Eddie asked.

Donald pulled out his notebook, which had been filled with increasingly complex business diagrams and competitive analysis since May. As he flipped through pages of organizational charts, pricing strategies, and expansion plans, he realized that all his strategic thinking had been focused on the same basic objective: building successful business ventures that would demonstrate his entrepreneurial capabilities.

"I've been trying to win," Donald said. "Beat the competition, make the most money, create the biggest events. But Franklin's been trying to help people."

Franklin honked softly from his pen, apparently understanding that he was being discussed.

"Franklin doesn't care about beating the Feinbergs," Donald continued. "He cares about whether Tommy Kowalski has fun at water balloon fights, whether Lisa gets the birthday party she wants, whether Mr. Chen's garden gets watered properly."

Donald felt the kind of recognition that came from understanding something important about success and relationships.

"Maybe," he said slowly, "instead of trying to compete with the Feinbergs, we should figure out what Franklin actually wants to do. What he's good at. What makes him happy."

Eddie and Frankie looked at Donald with surprise. This was the first time all summer that Donald had suggested prioritizing Franklin's preferences over business strategy.

"What do you think Franklin wants to do?" Frankie asked.

Donald closed his notebook and looked at Franklin, who was sitting quietly in his pen with the patient expression of someone waiting for important decisions to be made.

"Franklin," Donald called out, "if you could do anything you wanted, what would it be?"

Franklin stood up immediately and began honking in a pattern that Donald had learned indicated enthusiastic communication. Then Franklin performed his sitting trick and looked expectantly toward the fence that separated the Trump backyard from the rest of the neighbourhood.

"Franklin wants to visit people," Donald realized. "Not for business reasons. Just because he likes them."

Franklin honked agreement and honked again toward the fence, clearly indicating his desire to engage with the broader community.

"Franklin wants to be helpful," Donald continued, understanding Franklin's communication more clearly than he ever had before. "He wants to use his abilities to make people happy, not to make money."

This revelation required Donald to reconsider everything he'd learned about Franklin's motivations and abilities over the past month. Franklin's customer service excellence, his educational capabilities, his strategic intelligence, all of these had been expressions of Franklin's genuine desire to be helpful rather than profitable.

"So, what do we do?" Eddie asked.

Donald thought about this question for the rest of Monday and most of Tuesday. Franklin's desires for community engagement conflicted with Donald's grounding restrictions, but they also suggested a different approach to neighbourhood relationships that might address the concerns that had led to his current business suspension.

"Community service," Donald announced on Tuesday afternoon, having reached what he considered a strategic breakthrough. "Instead of competing with the Feinbergs on business terms, we collaborate with them on community improvement terms."

"Collaborate?" Frankie repeated.

"Franklin provides consultation services for community benefit rather than personal profit," Donald explained. "We work with the Feinbergs instead of against them, focusing on neighbourhood improvement that everyone can support."

This concept required Donald to abandon his competitive approach entirely and embrace what he was beginning to recognize as Franklin's natural inclination toward cooperative problem-solving.

"How do we collaborate with people who've been systematically out-competing us all summer?" Eddie asked.

Donald had been thinking about this challenge, and he'd developed what he hoped was a mature approach to competitive relationship management.

"We acknowledge that they're excellent at organization and efficiency," Donald said. "And we offer Franklin's consultation abilities as a complementary service that enhances their community programming rather than competing with it."

This was a significant strategic shift that required Donald to prioritize community benefit over personal competitive advantage, but he was beginning to understand that Franklin's approach to relationships was more sustainable than his own approach to business.

Wednesday morning, Donald made what he considered the most difficult business decision of his entrepreneurial career: he called the Feinberg twins and requested a meeting to discuss collaboration opportunities.

"Madeline? This is Donald Trump. I was wondering if you and Josephine might be interested in discussing some potential cooperation strategies that could benefit our entire neighbourhood community."

The pause on the other end of the line suggested that the twins were as surprised by Donald's collaborative overture as he was by making it.

"Cooperation strategies?" Madeline's voice carried the cautious tone of someone who suspected competitive trickery.

"Franklin's consultation abilities combined with your organizational capabilities," Donald explained. "Community service coordination that leverages everyone's strengths instead of creating competitive tension."

Another pause, followed by what sounded like consultation between the twins.

"We'll meet," Josephine's voice came on the line. "Thursday afternoon. Your backyard. Franklin present for strategic consultation."

Donald hung up the phone feeling like he'd just initiated the most important business negotiation of his summer, even though it wasn't really business anymore.

Thursday afternoon's meeting was the first time Donald had been in the same space as the Feinberg twins without feeling like he was being professionally evaluated for competitive weaknesses. Instead, he felt like he was participating in genuine strategic collaboration with people who shared similar goals.

"Your operation has been impressive," Madeline said, settling onto the picnic table bench with her matching notebook.

"Creative programming and unique service delivery," Josephine added, consulting her own notes about Donald's summer ventures.

"Thank you," Donald replied. "Your organizational capabilities have been... educational. I've learned a lot about systematic approach and professional efficiency."

This was diplomatically accurate. The twins had consistently demonstrated operational excellence that exceeded Donald's own strategic planning abilities.

Franklin, released from his pen for the meeting, approached the twins with his signature combination of dignity and friendliness. He performed his sitting trick and offered his hoof for formal introduction, which both twins accepted with obvious appreciation.

"Franklin's impressive," Madeline said, scratching behind Franklin's ears.

"Natural leadership abilities and genuine strategic intelligence," Josephine agreed.

Franklin honked acknowledgment and then, with typical initiative, began conducting what appeared to be his own assessment of collaboration opportunities.

Franklin positioned himself between Donald and the twins, honked twice for attention, and then performed a series of demonstrations that seemed designed to illustrate potential cooperative activities.

He showed how individual consultation (his specialty) could be combined with systematic organization (the twins' strength) to create comprehensive programming that served different customer needs simultaneously. He demonstrated how personal attention and efficient delivery could work together rather than compete against each other.

"Franklin's providing strategic collaboration consulting," Donald observed, watching his pig facilitate genuine communication between former competitors.

"Franklin understands that different approaches can be complementary rather than competitive," Madeline said.

"Operational diversity creates better service delivery for everyone," Josephine added.

Donald felt the kind of strategic breakthrough that came from understanding cooperation as a legitimate business strategy rather than just competitive positioning.

The meeting continued for two hours, with Franklin providing ongoing consultation while Donald and the twins developed what they called "comprehensive neighbourhood service coordination protocols."

The plan they developed was more ambitious than any of Donald's individual ventures, but also more sustainable because it distributed responsibilities according to actual capabilities rather than competitive positioning.

The Feinbergs would handle systematic delivery, organizational coordination, and efficient supply management. Donald and Franklin would provide personalized consultation, individual attention, and specialized problem-solving for customers who needed customized support.

"Different service offerings for different customer needs," Donald summarized. "Market diversity instead of market competition."

"Franklin's consultation abilities combined with our delivery capabilities," Madeline agreed.

"Comprehensive community service that nobody could provide individually," Josephine concluded.

Franklin honked enthusiastic approval and performed his sitting trick for all three human partners, apparently satisfied with the collaborative agreement.

Friday's test of the new collaboration model proved that cooperation was significantly more effective than competition for actually serving neighbourhood needs.

Their first joint project was organizing assistance for Mrs. Patterson, who'd been struggling with garden maintenance since her husband's business travel had increased. The Feinbergs provided systematic supply delivery and organizational coordination while Franklin offered personalized consultation about plant care and garden optimization.

"This is wonderful," Mrs. Patterson said, watching Franklin provide detailed horticultural advice while Madeline and Josephine efficiently distributed gardening supplies and coordinated work schedules. "I'm getting both professional organization and personal attention. Much better than trying to manage everything myself."

The collaboration generated genuine community benefit without any competitive tension, and Donald realized that working with the twins was considerably more satisfying than trying to defeat them.

"Franklin's happier," Eddie observed during Friday afternoon's assessment session. "He's not stressed about competitive positioning anymore. He's just focused on being helpful."

Donald watched Franklin provide individual consultation to Mr. Chen about optimal vegetable growing strategies while the twins coordinated neighbourhood supply sharing that made everyone's gardens more successful.

"I think I'm happier too," Donald admitted. "This feels like actual community service instead of just trying to prove something."

Friday evening brought validation that their collaborative approach was generating neighbourhood support rather than neighbourhood concern.

Mrs. Chen called to request joint services for Lisa's birthday party, the twins' organizational coordination combined with Franklin's personalized entertainment consultation.

"Lisa specifically asked for Franklin's individual attention," Mrs. Chen explained. "But she also wants the kind of organized activities that Madeline and Josephine provide. Could you work together on party planning?"

Donald felt the satisfaction that came from customer requests that recognized the value of collaborative service delivery.

"Franklin and I would be honoured to work with the Feinbergs on Lisa's party," Donald replied. "Comprehensive celebration planning that combines personalized consultation with professional organization."

Saturday's joint party planning session demonstrated that collaboration was not only more effective than competition but also more educational for everyone involved.

Franklin provided his characteristic individual attention to Lisa's party preferences, helping her identify activities that matched her personal interests and social objectives. The twins contributed systematic planning that ensured efficient party coordination, supply management, and guest experience optimization.

"This is the best party planning ever," Lisa declared, watching Franklin and the twins work together to design celebration activities that incorporated both personal attention and professional organization.

Donald served as coordination liaison between Franklin's consultation services and the twins' systematic planning, but he realized that his role was becoming more about facilitating collaboration than directing competitive strategy.

"Franklin's really good at understanding what people actually want," Madeline observed, watching Franklin adapt party recommendations based on Lisa's individual personality and interests.

"Donald's good at translating Franklin's insights into practical planning," Josephine added.

Donald felt recognized for abilities he hadn't known he possessed, not strategic business planning, but genuine communication and collaborative problem-solving.

"Maybe," Donald said, "we're all better at different things, and working together lets everyone contribute what they're actually good at."

Franklin honked enthusiastic agreement and performed his sitting trick for the entire collaborative planning team.

Sunday's reflection on the week's developments brought Donald to a recognition that changed his understanding of success entirely.

"Franklin," Donald said during their evening consultation session, "I think I've been thinking about business all wrong."

Franklin honked thoughtfully and looked at Donald with patient attention.

"I've been trying to beat other people instead of trying to help them," Donald continued. "But you've been focused on helping people all along. That's why everyone likes you better than they like my business strategies."

Franklin gently nudged Donald's hand with his snout, apparently offering encouragement for continued strategic thinking.

"What if," Donald said slowly, "instead of trying to build the biggest business or beat the most competition, we just focused on being genuinely helpful to people who need support?"

Franklin honked what sounded like enthusiastic approval.

"Not because it's profitable, but because it's the right thing to do."

Franklin performed his sitting trick and looked at Donald with what appeared to be pride.

As Donald settled Franklin in his pen that evening, he felt the kind of confidence that came from understanding genuine success rather than competitive advantage.

Of course, he didn't yet know that Mrs. Henderson's "concerned neighbour coordination" had decided that collaborative activities were acceptable community programming, or that Lisa's birthday party would provide an opportunity to demonstrate the kind of authentic friendship that Franklin had been teaching all summer.

But those were tomorrow's opportunities. Tonight, Donald had discovered that his pig was capable of genuine collaboration and authentic service, and that those qualities were more valuable than any competitive business strategy.

Franklin honked goodnight, and Donald fell asleep planning community service that would focus on helping neighbours rather than beating competition.

He still had no idea that the real reward for authentic friendship was about to become clear.

The Unlikely Alliance

Lisa Chen's birthday party was scheduled for Saturday afternoon, and by Thursday morning, Donald was experiencing a completely new type of pre-event anxiety. For the first time all summer, he wasn't worried about competitive advantage, profit margins, or strategic positioning. Instead, he was worried about whether he and Franklin could actually deliver the kind of genuine friendship and authentic support that Lisa deserved.

"What if we mess this up?" Donald asked Franklin during Thursday morning's planning session. "What if collaboration doesn't work as well as competition? What if Lisa's party isn't as good as it would have been if the twins organized it alone?"

Franklin honked thoughtfully and performed his sitting trick, which Donald had learned to interpret as patient encouragement for continued strategic thinking.

"The problem is," Donald continued, "I've gotten good at organizing business ventures and competitive positioning. But I'm not sure I know how to just be a friend who helps plan a party."

Franklin approached Donald and gently nudged his hand, apparently offering support for Donald's uncertainty about authentic relationship management.

"Franklin," Donald said, "you've been trying to teach me about friendship all summer, haven't you?"

Franklin honked what sounded like confirmation.

"And I've been so focused on business success that I missed the actual point of having a business partner who cares about people."

Franklin performed his sitting trick and looked at Donald with what appeared to be patience and understanding.

Donald spent Thursday afternoon reviewing his notebook, but instead of studying competitive strategies and expansion plans, he was trying to understand what Franklin had been demonstrating about genuine service and authentic attention.

"Franklin doesn't provide consultation because it's profitable," Donald realized during Thursday evening's reflection session. "He provides consultation because he genuinely cares whether people get what they need."

This understanding required Donald to reconsider every interaction he'd observed between Franklin and neighbourhood customers over the past month. Franklin's garden advice for Mr. Chen, his tactical training for water balloon participants, his individual attention for children who needed extra support, all of these had been expressions of authentic care rather than strategic business positioning.

"Franklin," Donald said, "I think you've been running a friendship operation while I thought we were running a business enterprise."

Franklin honked agreement and gently nudged Donald's notebook, apparently suggesting that strategic planning should focus on friendship objectives rather than competitive positioning.

Friday morning's final preparation session with the Feinberg twins confirmed that collaboration was going to require Donald to develop entirely new skills in cooperative planning and shared decision-making.

"Lisa's requested three specific party elements," Madeline reported, consulting her notes about the birthday celebration requirements. "Swimming activities, creative projects, and what she calls 'Franklin time.'"

"Franklin time?" Donald asked.

"Individual consultation and personal attention," Josephine explained. "Lisa specifically wants time to talk with Franklin about things that are important to her."

Donald felt the kind of responsibility that came from understanding that someone genuinely valued Franklin's friendship and was counting on Donald to facilitate authentic connection rather than entertainment programming.

"Franklin can definitely provide individual consultation," Donald said. "But I want to make sure we're creating genuine friendship interaction rather than just scheduled entertainment activities."

The twins exchanged glances that suggested they were reassessing Donald's approach to party planning.

"You're prioritizing Lisa's actual preferences over programmatic efficiency?" Madeline asked.

"Franklin's taught me that authentic relationships are more important than systematic programming," Donald replied. "Lisa should get the kind of party that makes her happy, not the kind of party that demonstrates our organizational capabilities."

Franklin honked approval and performed his sitting trick for the collaborative planning team, apparently satisfied with Donald's friendship-focused strategic adjustment.

Friday afternoon's venue preparation at the Chen house demonstrated that cooperative planning was significantly more effective than competitive positioning for actually creating celebration experiences that guests would enjoy.

The twins handled systematic party infrastructure, table arrangements, supply organization, activity coordination, with their characteristic efficiency. Donald and Franklin focused on personalized consultation, understanding Lisa's individual preferences, adapting activities to her personality, and ensuring that celebration elements reflected her genuine interests rather than standard party programming.

"This feels different from business party planning," Donald observed to Eddie and Frankie as they watched Franklin provide consultation about optimal swimming activity coordination while the twins organized efficient supply distribution.

"It feels like we're actually creating something Lisa wants instead of something that proves how good we are at organizing parties," Eddie replied.

Franklin honked agreement and continued his detailed consultation with Lisa about birthday celebration preferences that reflected her individual personality and social objectives.

"Franklin really listens," Lisa told Donald during Friday afternoon's planning session. "He pays attention to what I actually want instead of just assuming he knows what would be fun."

Donald watched Franklin adapt party recommendations based on Lisa's specific feedback and realized that Franklin's greatest ability was authentic attention, genuinely caring about individual preferences and responding thoughtfully to personal needs.

"Franklin's taught me that real service means understanding what people actually want," Donald said. "Not what I think they should want, or what's most profitable, or what beats the competition. Just what actually makes them happy."

Saturday morning dawned clear and warm, perfect birthday party weather. Donald spent the early hours completing final preparation and reviewing what he now thought of as "friendship protocols" rather than business strategies.

Franklin had been groomed and prepared for his individual consultation responsibilities, but Donald noticed that Franklin seemed more relaxed and confident than he'd been during previous party events. Franklin was approaching Lisa's birthday with genuine enthusiasm rather than professional obligation.

"Franklin's excited about this party," Donald told his parents during Saturday morning's operational briefing. "Not because it's business, but because he genuinely likes Lisa and wants her to have a good birthday."

Mrs. Trump looked at Donald with the expression of someone who was recognizing important personal development. "Donald, you sound different when you talk about this party. Less worried about proving something and more focused on making sure Lisa has fun."

"Franklin's taught me that helping people is more satisfying than beating people," Donald replied. "Even when helping people doesn't generate competitive advantage or profit margins."

The party began at two o'clock with what Donald immediately recognized as the most successful collaborative event of his summer. The twins' systematic organization created smooth party coordination while Franklin provided the individual attention that made each guest feel personally valued and included.

Lisa was clearly delighted by the combination of efficient programming and authentic personal consultation. She participated enthusiastically in organized activities while also spending time with Franklin discussing things that were important to her individually.

"This is the best birthday party ever," Lisa announced during the afternoon swimming session, where Franklin was providing aquatic supervision while the twins coordinated group games and Donald managed guest relations.

Donald felt the satisfaction that came from successful cooperation rather than competitive victory. Everyone was contributing their actual strengths, and Lisa was receiving celebration experiences that none of them could have provided individually.

The afternoon's success was enhanced by Franklin's natural ability to adapt his consultation approach to different guests' individual needs. He provided strategic advice to children who wanted game coordination, offered patient attention to guests who preferred quiet conversation, and demonstrated his swimming abilities for participants who wanted aquatic entertainment.

"Franklin's like having the perfect party guest," observed Mrs. Chen, watching Franklin move easily between different groups while providing exactly the kind of interaction that each guest appreciated.

"Franklin understands that different people want different kinds of attention," Donald realized. "He doesn't try to provide the same service to everyone. He pays attention to what each person actually enjoys."

This insight about Franklin's approach to individual relationships applied equally to Donald's understanding of business cooperation. Instead of trying to compete with the twins' systematic capabilities, Donald was learning to contribute his own strengths while appreciating their organizational excellence.

"Collaboration is more effective than competition for actually serving people's needs," Donald told Eddie and Frankie during a brief operational assessment while Franklin provided swimming consultation to guests who wanted aquatic strategic advice.

"And it's more fun," Frankie added. "Nobody's stressed about beating anyone else. Everyone's just focused on making sure Lisa has a good party."

The afternoon's highlight came when Lisa specifically requested what she called "Franklin consultation time", individual conversation with Franklin about things that were important to her beyond party activities.

Donald watched Lisa and Franklin settle into a quiet corner of the backyard for what appeared to be genuine personal conversation. Franklin listened attentively while Lisa talked, honked thoughtful responses, and occasionally performed his sitting trick when Lisa said something that seemed to particularly resonate with him.

"What are they talking about?" Eddie asked.

"I don't know," Donald replied. "But Franklin's providing the kind of individual attention that Lisa wanted, and that's what matters."

Donald realized that Franklin's consultation with Lisa wasn't about party planning or strategic coordination, it was about genuine friendship between two individuals who enjoyed each other's company and appreciated authentic personal connection.

"Franklin's not just a business partner," Donald said, understanding something fundamental about relationships and success. "He's actually a friend who happens to be helpful with business activities."

This recognition changed Donald's understanding of his entire summer experience. All of Franklin's customer service excellence, strategic intelligence, and community engagement had been expressions of Franklin's natural inclination toward friendship rather than commercial success.

The party concluded at five o'clock with what everyone agreed was the most successful birthday celebration the neighbourhood had seen all summer. Lisa was clearly delighted with her party, guests had enjoyed both organized activities and individual attention, and parents were impressed by the collaborative organization that had created celebration experiences without competitive tension.

"This was wonderful," Mrs. Chen told Donald as the party wound down. "Lisa got exactly the kind of celebration she wanted, and everyone worked together to make it happen. Much better than having competing party planning services."

Donald felt the satisfaction that came from successful collaboration rather than competitive victory. "Franklin taught me that helping people is more important than beating people," he said. "And working with the twins is more effective than trying to compete with them."

"Lisa's very fond of Franklin," Mrs. Chen continued. "And I think Franklin's good for her. He provides the kind of patient attention that helps children feel genuinely valued."

As Donald and Franklin walked home that evening, Donald felt confident that he'd learned something essential about authentic success and genuine relationships.

"Franklin," Donald said, "I think this was the first time all summer that we focused on what you're actually good at instead of what I thought would be profitable."

Franklin honked agreement and performed his sitting trick.

"And it worked better than any of my business strategies," Donald continued. "You were happier, Lisa was happier, everyone was happier. Even me."

Franklin gently nudged Donald's hand and honked what sounded like encouragement for continued friendship-focused thinking.

As Donald settled Franklin in his pen that evening, he felt the kind of confidence that came from understanding collaboration and authentic service rather than competitive positioning.

But Sunday morning brought a development that would test Donald's newfound commitment to cooperation over competition in ways he hadn't anticipated.

Mrs. Henderson called to request what she diplomatically described as "community problem-solving assistance" for a situation that involved "neighbourhood cooperation and individual consultation requirements."

"What kind of problem?" Donald asked, though Mrs. Henderson's formal tone suggested that this wasn't a simple party planning request.

"The Morrison family is moving next week," Mrs. Henderson explained. "They've asked for help with yard sale organization, moving coordination, and what Mrs. Morrison specifically called 'Franklin's consultation services for helping children adjust to major life changes.'"

Donald felt the kind of responsibility that came from being asked to provide genuine support for people experiencing actual difficulties rather than just entertainment for summer recreation.

"Franklin and I would be honoured to help," Donald said. "We'll coordinate with the Feinbergs to provide comprehensive assistance for whatever the Morrison family needs."

"Donald," Mrs. Henderson said, and her tone carried a warmth that Donald hadn't heard from her since before the garage sale incident, "I appreciate the mature approach you and Franklin have developed. The neighbourhood has noticed the difference in your recent activities."

Donald hung up the phone feeling like he'd received recognition for personal growth rather than business achievement.

"Franklin," Donald told his pig during Sunday afternoon's consultation session, "I think we might have finally figured out what we're actually supposed to be doing."

Franklin honked thoughtful agreement and looked toward the fence that separated them from the rest of the neighbourhood, not with the ambitious energy of previous business ventures, but with the patient attention of someone who understood genuine service opportunities.

"Next week," Donald said, "we help a family with one of the most difficult things that happens to people. Moving away from their community and friends."

Franklin honked seriously and performed his sitting trick, apparently understanding the importance of the assistance they'd been asked to provide.

As Donald planned consultation services that would focus on authentic support rather than profitable entertainment, he felt the kind of confidence that came from understanding genuine success.

The summer was far from over, but Donald finally understood what Franklin had been trying to teach him about the difference between competitive achievement and authentic friendship.

Franklin honked goodnight, and Donald fell asleep planning community service that would help people through difficult transitions rather than just providing entertainment for summer recreation.

He still had no idea that helping the Morrison family would lead to the most important friendship lesson of his entire summer.

County Fair Comeback

The Morrison family's moving crisis had lasted four days, and by Thursday evening, Donald understood something about genuine service that all his business planning had never taught him. Real help, the kind that actually mattered, wasn't about entertainment or profit or competitive advantage. It was about showing up when things were difficult and staying until the problem was solved, even when staying wasn't fun or profitable or strategically advantageous.

Franklin had provided consultation services that exceeded anything Donald had imagined possible. He'd helped eight-year-old Jenny Morrison process the emotional complexity of leaving her friends and familiar neighbourhood. He'd offered patient attention to ten-year-old Marcus Morrison, who was worried about making new friends and fitting into a different school. He'd even provided what appeared to be genuine therapeutic support to Mrs. Morrison, who was struggling with the logistics of coordinating a cross-country move while managing two children's emotional needs.

"Franklin understands that moving is scary," Jenny Morrison had told Donald on Wednesday afternoon, sitting next to Franklin's pen while the pig listened to her concerns about leaving her best friends behind. "He makes me feel like everything's going to be okay."

Donald had watched Franklin provide four hours of patient attention to a little girl who needed someone to listen to her worries without trying to fix them or make them go away. Franklin didn't offer solutions or strategic advice, he simply sat with Jenny and let her talk about being afraid and sad and excited all at the same time.

"This is what you've been trying to teach me," Donald had said to Franklin that evening. "That sometimes the most helpful thing you can do is just be present when people need support."

Franklin had honked softly and performed his sitting trick, apparently satisfied that Donald was finally understanding genuine service priorities.

The Morrison family had left Thursday morning with a yard sale that raised enough money to cover their moving expenses, a house that was cleaned and organized for the new owners, and two children who felt confident about their family's transition because Franklin had helped them understand that being scared about changes was normal and that they could handle whatever came next.

"Thank you," Mrs. Morrison had said to Donald as she loaded the last boxes into their moving truck. "Franklin provided exactly the kind of support that Jenny and Marcus needed. You should be proud of what you've both accomplished."

Donald had felt the kind of satisfaction that came from genuine service rather than competitive achievement. But he'd also realized that helping the Morrison family had changed his understanding of success in ways that made his previous business ventures seem somehow smaller and less important.

"Franklin," Donald said during Thursday evening's reflection session, "I think we might have graduated from summer business ventures into something more important."

Franklin honked thoughtful agreement and looked toward the fence that separated them from the neighbourhood, but not with the ambitious energy of previous entrepreneurial planning. Instead,

Franklin seemed to be considering genuine service opportunities that might exist throughout their community.

"The question is," Donald continued, "what do we do with what we've learned? How do we use Franklin's friendship abilities and my organizational skills to actually help people instead of just entertaining them?"

Friday morning brought an answer to Donald's question in the form of an unexpected visitor: Mr. Peterson from the county extension office, who arrived at the Trump house with what he described as "a community service opportunity that might interest young people with demonstrated organizational abilities and animal management experience."

Donald answered the door wearing his regular clothes, he'd stopped wearing his father's suits after the Independence Day incident, and found himself facing a middle-aged man in work clothes who carried himself with the practical authority of someone who spent his time solving real problems.

"You're Donald Trump?" Mr. Peterson asked. "The young man who's been organizing neighbourhood activities with the assistance of a pig?"

"Yes, sir," Donald replied, though he wondered how news of Franklin's consultation services had reached the county extension office.

"Mrs. Chen called our office yesterday," Mr. Peterson explained. "She mentioned that you and your pig have been providing what she called 'genuine community service' and that you might be interested in participating in our annual county fair volunteer program."

Donald felt immediate interest. The county fair was serious business, real agriculture, genuine competition, and community celebration that attracted families from throughout the region. Participation would mean Franklin's abilities being recognized beyond their immediate neighbourhood.

"What kind of volunteer program?" Donald asked.

"We need assistance with children's educational programming," Mr. Peterson said. "Specifically, we're looking for young people who can help coordinate activities that teach children about agriculture, animal care, and community cooperation. Mrs. Chen mentioned that your pig has demonstrated remarkable abilities in individual consultation and group activity coordination."

Franklin, hearing his name mentioned, approached the front porch and honked politely at Mr. Peterson.

"So, this is Franklin," Mr. Peterson said, clearly impressed by Franklin's dignified greeting behaviour. "Mrs. Chen was right about his social intelligence. That's exactly the kind of animal presence that makes our educational programming successful."

Donald felt the kind of recognition that came from having Franklin's genuine abilities acknowledged by adults who understood the difference between entertainment and education.

"What would our responsibilities be?" Donald asked.

"Educational consultation for children who want to learn about animal care, agricultural principles, and community cooperation," Mr. Peterson explained. "We provide the programmatic structure, and you provide individual attention and personalized consultation that helps children connect with agricultural concepts."

Donald looked at Franklin, who was listening to the conversation with obvious interest and occasionally honking what sounded like questions about the volunteer opportunity.

"Franklin would be working with children who are genuinely interested in learning?" Donald asked.

"Children and families who specifically request individual consultation services," Mr. Peterson confirmed. "We've found that some children learn better through personal attention and customized explanation rather than group programming. Your pig's consultation abilities could provide exactly the kind of individualized support that makes our educational mission successful."

Donald felt the excitement that came from recognizing genuine opportunity for meaningful service rather than just profitable entertainment.

"We'd be honoured to participate," Donald said. "Franklin's consultation services are available for any educational programming that would benefit children and families."

Mr. Peterson smiled and shook Donald's hand with the respect accorded to someone who'd just committed to genuine community service. "The fair runs from Friday through Sunday next week. Can you provide consultation services for all three days?"

"Franklin and I will be there," Donald promised.

Friday evening's preparation for county fair participation required Donald to reconsider his entire approach to event planning and community service. Instead of developing competitive strategies and profit optimization, Donald found himself focusing on Franklin's consultation abilities and how they could best serve families who were genuinely interested in agricultural education.

"This is different from neighbourhood party planning," Donald told Eddie and Frankie during Friday's briefing session. "These are families who specifically want educational consultation about farming and animal care. Franklin needs to provide genuine information, not just entertainment."

Franklin honked seriously and performed his sitting trick, apparently understanding the increased responsibility involved in educational programming for families who were counting on accurate information and helpful consultation.

"What if people ask Franklin about things he doesn't know?" Eddie asked.

Donald had been considering this challenge, and he'd developed what he hoped was an appropriate approach to consultation ethics and educational responsibility.

"Franklin provides consultation about things he genuinely understands," Donald said. "Animal behaviour, social interaction, individual attention, and problem-solving approaches. If families need technical agricultural information, we refer them to Mr. Peterson and the official county extension experts."

This seemed like a reasonable division of consultation responsibilities that would allow Franklin to contribute his authentic abilities while ensuring that families received accurate technical information from qualified sources.

Saturday morning's departure for the county fair marked the first time all summer that Donald was participating in organized activities without feeling competitive anxiety about performance outcomes or business success metrics.

"Franklin," Donald said as they loaded Franklin's transportation crate into his father's car, "this is your chance to provide consultation services for families who really need what you're good at. No business pressure, no competitive positioning, just helping people learn things they want to know."

Franklin honked agreement and settled into his crate with the calm confidence of someone who understood his responsibilities and was looking forward to meaningful work.

The county fair was larger and more impressive than Donald had expected. Acres of agricultural displays, genuine farm animals, educational exhibits, and families from throughout the region participating in celebration of rural community values and agricultural traditions.

"This is serious farming," Donald observed as Mr. Peterson led them through the fair grounds toward their assigned educational area. "Real agriculture with families who understand animal care and community cooperation."

Franklin, released from his crate, surveyed the fair environment with obvious fascination. He honked politely at passing farm animals, performed his sitting trick for children who stopped to observe him, and generally conducted himself with the professional dignity appropriate for genuine educational programming.

"Franklin's ready for advanced consultation responsibilities," Donald told Mr. Peterson as they reached their assigned area, a section designated for individual educational consultation and personalized learning support.

"Let's see how he handles his first consultation request," Mr. Peterson replied.

Their first consultation opportunity came within minutes. A family with three young children approached their area specifically requesting individual consultation about animal care and farming principles.

"We heard about Franklin's educational abilities," the mother explained. "Our children are interested in learning about responsible animal ownership, and we understand that Franklin provides personalized consultation that helps children understand animal behaviour and care requirements."

Donald felt the kind of responsibility that came from families who were counting on genuine educational service rather than just entertainment programming.

"Franklin provides consultation about animal social intelligence, individual personality recognition, and relationship-building principles," Donald explained. "He helps children understand that animals are individuals with their own preferences and needs."

Franklin approached the three children with his characteristic combination of dignity and friendliness. He offered his hoof for formal introduction, performed his sitting trick to establish his consultation credentials, and then began what appeared to be systematic individual assessment of each child's interests and learning preferences.

The oldest child, a girl of about ten, was clearly interested in technical animal care information. Franklin provided consultation about proper feeding procedures, appropriate exercise requirements, and social interaction principles through a combination of demonstration and what Donald was learning to recognize as Franklin's natural teaching methods.

The middle child, a boy of about eight, was more interested in animal behaviour and personality understanding. Franklin adapted his consultation approach to focus on animal communication principles, individual attention requirements, and relationship-building strategies that helped the boy understand animals as individuals rather than just pets.

The youngest child, a girl of about six, was primarily interested in whether animals could be friends with people. Franklin's consultation for her focused on demonstrating genuine friendship through patient attention, gentle interaction, and the kind of authentic care that made the little girl feel comfortable and valued.

"Franklin's providing three different consultation approaches for three different learning needs," Donald observed to the children's parents, who were watching the educational session with obvious appreciation.

"He's responding to what each child is actually interested in learning," the father replied. "That's exactly the kind of individualized education we were hoping for."

Donald watched Franklin spend forty-five minutes providing personalized consultation that adapted to each child's questions, concerns, and learning style, and realized that Franklin's educational abilities exceeded anything he'd witnessed during neighbourhood entertainment programming.

"Franklin understands that different people learn differently," Donald said. "He provides consultation that matches individual needs rather than standard programming."

The family left with genuine agricultural education, satisfied consultation experiences, and requests for Franklin's contact information for future learning support. More importantly, the children had clearly developed understanding of animal care principles that would serve them well in future agricultural activities.

"That was impressive consultation work," Mr. Peterson told Donald as they prepared for their next educational opportunity. "Franklin demonstrates natural teaching abilities that complement our programmatic offerings perfectly."

The morning continued with a steady stream of families requesting Franklin's individual consultation services. Each consultation was different, reflecting the specific interests and learning needs of different children and families, but all resulted in genuine educational value and customer satisfaction that exceeded standard fair programming.

"Franklin's consultation services are generating requests faster than we can schedule them," Donald reported to Mr. Peterson during the midday operational assessment. "Families are specifically asking for personalized educational support that adapts to individual learning preferences."

"Franklin's filling a genuine educational need," Mr. Peterson replied. "Many children learn better through individual attention and customized explanation than through group programming. Franklin's natural teaching abilities provide exactly the kind of personalized support that makes our educational mission successful."

Donald felt the satisfaction that came from contributing genuine value to community educational programming rather than just providing entertainment for summer recreation.

The afternoon brought Franklin's most challenging consultation opportunity: a family with a twelve-year-old boy who had been diagnosed with what his parents described as "social interaction difficulties" and who was interested in learning about animal care as a potential therapeutic activity.

"Michael has trouble with group activities and conventional social interaction," the boy's mother explained to Donald. "But he's very interested in animals, and we thought Franklin's individual consultation approach might help him understand animal relationship principles that could transfer to human social interaction."

Donald felt the kind of responsibility that came from being asked to provide consultation for genuine therapeutic support rather than simple educational entertainment.

"Franklin specializes in individual attention and personalized relationship building," Donald said. "He understands that different people need different kinds of social interaction, and he adapts his consultation approach to whatever makes people feel comfortable and valued."

Franklin approached Michael with his characteristic patience and dignity, but Donald noticed that Franklin's consultation approach was different from his previous educational sessions. Instead of beginning with formal introductions and demonstration activities, Franklin simply positioned himself near Michael and waited for the boy to initiate interaction according to his own comfort level.

Michael was clearly interested in Franklin but uncertain about appropriate social interaction protocols. Franklin solved this by performing his sitting trick and then remaining perfectly still, allowing Michael to observe and approach at his own pace without any pressure for immediate social engagement.

"Franklin understands that social interaction should happen naturally," Donald observed to Michael's parents, who were watching the consultation with obvious concern and hope.

"He's not pushing Michael to interact faster than feels comfortable," the mother replied. "That's exactly what Michael needs, someone who respects his individual social timing."

Donald watched Franklin provide thirty minutes of patient presence while Michael gradually became comfortable with closer proximity and eventual gentle physical interaction. Franklin's consultation didn't focus on teaching specific animal care techniques, instead, Franklin demonstrated that relationships could develop naturally when both individuals respected each other's preferences and boundaries.

"Franklin's teaching Michael that friendship doesn't have to follow standard social rules," Donald realized. "It can develop according to individual personalities and comfort levels."

By the end of the consultation session, Michael was sitting comfortably next to Franklin, providing gentle pets and scratches while Franklin honked soft responses that clearly indicated enjoyment and appreciation for Michael's individual attention.

"This is the best animal interaction Michael has had," his father told Donald as the consultation concluded. "Franklin's approach helps Michael understand that relationships can be genuine and supportive without requiring conventional social performance."

Donald felt the kind of recognition that came from understanding Franklin's greatest ability: creating authentic connection with people who needed individual attention and customized relationship approaches.

"Franklin provides consultation that adapts to individual needs," Donald said. "He doesn't expect people to fit standard social patterns. He works with whatever makes people feel comfortable and valued."

The family left with genuine educational value, therapeutic progress, and requests for continued consultation support that could provide ongoing relationship development assistance for Michael's social interaction learning.

"That was exceptional consultation work," Mr. Peterson told Donald as they concluded Saturday's educational programming. "Franklin's individual attention abilities provide exactly the kind of personalized support that makes genuine educational difference for children with special learning needs."

Saturday evening's reflection on the day's consultation experiences brought Donald to a recognition that changed his understanding of Franklin's abilities and his own role in community service.

"Franklin," Donald said during their evening session, "you're not just good at entertainment or business consultation. You're actually good at helping people with real problems that matter to their lives."

Franklin honked thoughtful agreement and looked at Donald with patient attention.

"And I think," Donald continued, "maybe that's what I want to be good at too. Not just organizing profitable activities, but actually helping people with things that are important to them."

Franklin performed his sitting trick and honked what sounded like encouragement for Donald's evolving understanding of authentic service priorities.

Sunday's final day of county fair consultation provided confirmation that Franklin's educational abilities and Donald's organizational skills could create genuine community value when focused on authentic service rather than competitive positioning.

Their morning consultation requests included families with children interested in agricultural careers, parents seeking advice about introducing pets into their households, and what Mr. Peterson described as "therapeutic consultation for children who benefit from animal-assisted emotional support."

"Franklin's consultation services are providing educational value that extends beyond simple agricultural information," Mr. Peterson observed during Sunday morning's briefing. "He's helping families understand relationship principles, individual attention requirements, and community cooperation concepts that apply to many aspects of life."

Donald felt proud of Franklin's expanding educational impact, but he also realized that Franklin's abilities were revealing opportunities for community service that exceeded anything Donald had originally imagined.

"Franklin's teaching people things they need to know about relationships and cooperation," Donald said. "Not just farming or animal care, but how to pay attention to individual needs and provide authentic support for people who are struggling with difficulties."

The morning's highlight came when a family specifically requested consultation about "animal-assisted community service" for their teenage daughter, who was interested in developing volunteer programs that used animal interaction to support children with social or emotional difficulties.

"Sarah wants to create therapeutic programming that helps children through animal relationship experiences," the girl's mother explained. "We heard about Franklin's individual consultation abilities and wondered if he could provide strategic advice about effective animal-assisted community service."

Donald felt the kind of recognition that came from families who understood Franklin's genuine capabilities and wanted to learn from his natural therapeutic instincts.

Franklin's consultation with sixteen-year-old Sarah lasted nearly two hours and covered topics that Donald recognized as sophisticated community service planning. Franklin demonstrated individual attention techniques, showed how to adapt interaction approaches to different personality types, and provided what appeared to be genuine strategic consultation about creating therapeutic programming that would serve children with special emotional or social needs.

"Franklin really understands how to help people feel valued and supported," Sarah told Donald as the consultation concluded. "He's teaching me approaches to individual attention that I never would have thought of on my own."

Donald watched Sarah take detailed notes about Franklin's consultation recommendations and realized that Franklin was providing educational value that could multiply throughout the community as Sarah developed her own therapeutic programming based on Franklin's natural relationship principles.

"Franklin's not just helping individual families," Donald understood. "He's teaching people to help other people. His consultation services are creating community service capabilities that will continue helping people even when Franklin's not directly involved."

Sunday afternoon's final consultation opportunity brought Donald face-to-face with a recognition that would shape his understanding of genuine success for the rest of his life.

A family approached their consultation area with a specific request that surprised Donald with its directness and importance.

"We heard about Franklin's consultation services from the Morrison family," the father explained. "Our son is starting high school next month, and he's struggling with confidence and social anxiety. Mrs. Morrison said that Franklin provides the kind of individual attention that helps children understand their own capabilities and feel confident about handling new situations."

Donald looked at the fifteen-year-old boy, who was clearly nervous about requesting consultation but equally clearly hoping that Franklin could provide support for challenges that felt overwhelming and important.

"Franklin specializes in individual confidence consultation," Donald said, though he realized he was describing abilities that Franklin had developed naturally rather than through any training or strategic planning.

Franklin approached the teenager with his characteristic patience and dignity, but Donald noticed that Franklin's consultation approach was adapting to the young man's age and specific needs. Instead of beginning with entertainment or demonstration activities, Franklin simply sat near the teenager and waited for natural conversation to develop.

"I'm worried about starting high school," the teenager said quietly to Franklin. "Everyone else seems to know how to be confident and popular, but I don't understand how social interaction works."

Franklin honked softly and gently nudged the teenager's hand, apparently offering support for concerns that clearly felt serious and important.

"Franklin understands that social confidence develops naturally when you focus on being genuinely helpful rather than trying to impress people," Donald found himself saying, though he realized he was describing lessons that Franklin had been teaching him all summer.

"How do you know when you're being genuinely helpful?" the teenager asked.

Donald looked at Franklin, who was providing patient attention and authentic presence that clearly made the teenager feel valued and supported.

"You pay attention to what people actually need," Donald said, understanding this principle for the first time in his life. "Not what you think they should need, or what's most profitable, or what makes you look good. Just what actually helps them feel better or solve their problems."

Franklin honked agreement and performed his sitting trick for the teenager, apparently demonstrating the kind of authentic attention that creates genuine confidence and social connection.

The consultation continued for an hour, with Franklin providing patient support while Donald found himself offering strategic advice about social interaction that reflected everything Franklin had taught him about authentic relationship building.

"Franklin's teaching me that confidence comes from caring about other people rather than worrying about what other people think of you," the teenager said as the consultation concluded.

Donald realized that Franklin had just provided therapeutic support that helped someone his own age understand principles that Donald was still learning about genuine confidence and authentic social success.

"Franklin's consultation services help people understand their own capabilities," Donald told the teenager's parents as the family prepared to leave. "He demonstrates that genuine social confidence develops when you focus on being helpful and authentic rather than trying to perform or compete."

The family left with what appeared to be genuine therapeutic value, practical strategies for social confidence development, and requests for continued consultation support that could provide ongoing guidance during the teenager's high school transition.

"That was exceptional consultation work," Mr. Peterson told Donald as they concluded Sunday's educational programming. "Franklin's individual attention abilities provide therapeutic value that extends far beyond agricultural education. He's helping people understand relationship principles and personal confidence concepts that apply to many aspects of community life."

Sunday evening's reflection on the county fair experience brought Donald to a recognition that would define his understanding of genuine success and authentic community service.

"Franklin," Donald said during their evening consultation session, "this weekend you provided educational services that actually helped people with problems that matter to their lives. Real therapeutic value, not just entertainment."

Franklin honked thoughtfully and looked at Donald with patient attention.

"And I think," Donald continued, "maybe this is what we're actually supposed to be doing. Not trying to build profitable businesses or beat competitive challenges, but using Franklin's abilities and my organizational skills to provide genuine support for people who need help with important difficulties."

Franklin performed his sitting trick and honked what sounded like enthusiastic agreement with Donald's strategic reassessment.

"The question is," Donald said, "how do we continue providing this kind of community service when we get home? How do we use what we've learned about authentic help to serve our own neighbourhood in ways that actually matter?"

Franklin honked toward the direction of home and performed his sitting trick again, apparently indicating his readiness to continue genuine consultation services for their community.

As Donald settled Franklin for the night in the fair's temporary animal housing, he felt the kind of confidence that came from understanding meaningful work rather than competitive achievement.

Monday morning's return to the neighbourhood brought immediate confirmation that Franklin's county fair consultation services had generated recognition throughout the broader community.

"Donald!" Mrs. Chen called out as Donald and Franklin walked up their street from his father's car. "How was the county fair? We heard wonderful things about Franklin's educational programming."

"Franklin provided consultation services for families who needed individual attention and personalized learning support," Donald replied. "He helped children understand animal care principles, relationship development, and social confidence concepts."

"That sounds like exactly the kind of community service that makes a real difference," Mrs. Chen said. "Lisa's been telling everyone about Franklin's friendship abilities and how much his individual attention has meant to her personal confidence development."

Donald felt the kind of recognition that came from community appreciation for genuine service rather than competitive business achievement.

"Mrs. Chen," Donald said, "would you be interested in helping us develop ongoing consultation services for neighbourhood families who might benefit from Franklin's individual attention abilities?"

"What kind of consultation services?" Mrs. Chen asked.

"Therapeutic support for children who are struggling with confidence or social difficulties," Donald explained. "Educational assistance for families who want personalized learning approaches. Individual attention for people who need someone to listen carefully and respond thoughtfully to their concerns."

Mrs. Chen considered this proposal while Franklin honked politely and performed his sitting trick to demonstrate his consultation credentials.

"That sounds like genuine community service," Mrs. Chen said. "How would you organize that kind of programming?"

Donald looked at Franklin, who was listening to the conversation with obvious interest and occasionally honking what sounded like strategic consultation about community service development.

"Collaboration with families who understand Franklin's capabilities," Donald said. "Working with parents like you who appreciate individual attention and authentic relationship building. Creating consultation opportunities that serve real needs rather than just providing entertainment."

Monday afternoon's planning session with Eddie, Frankie, and the Feinberg twins demonstrated that Donald's county fair experience had provided strategic clarity about genuine community service that could guide their collaborative efforts throughout the remaining summer.

"Franklin's consultation abilities are valuable for therapeutic support, educational assistance, and individual attention that helps people with real difficulties," Donald explained to the collaborative planning team. "Instead of focusing on entertainment or profit, we should focus on creating consultation services that actually help people solve problems that matter to their lives."

Madeline and Josephine exchanged glances that suggested they were recognizing Donald's genuine strategic evolution rather than just competitive repositioning.

"Community service consultation that combines Franklin's individual attention with our organizational capabilities?" Madeline asked.

"Therapeutic support that helps families while building authentic neighbourhood relationships," Josephine added.

Franklin honked enthusiastic agreement and performed his sitting trick for the entire collaborative team, apparently satisfied with the community service strategic direction.

"What we learned at the county fair," Donald continued, "is that Franklin's abilities provide genuine value for people who need individual support, personalized attention, and authentic relationship building. If we can organize consultation services that connect Franklin with families who need what he's good at, we can provide community service that actually makes a difference."

The collaborative planning session continued for two hours, with Franklin providing ongoing consultation while Donald and the twins developed what they called "comprehensive neighbourhood therapeutic support programming."

The plan they developed was more ambitious than any of Donald's individual business ventures, but also more meaningful because it focused on serving genuine community needs rather than generating competitive advantage or profitable entertainment.

"Franklin's Individual Consultation Services," Donald announced as they concluded Monday's planning session. "Therapeutic support, educational assistance, and authentic relationship building for families who need personalized attention and individual care."

Franklin honked official approval and performed his sitting trick for the entire collaborative team.

Monday evening's conversation with his parents about the county fair experience and future community service plans brought Donald to the most important strategic discussion of his summer.

"Mom, Dad," Donald said, joining his parents in the living room after dinner, "I want to talk about what Franklin and I learned at the county fair and how we want to use that experience for genuine community service."

Fred and Mary Trump looked at their son with the attention that suggested they were recognizing important personal development rather than just summer activity planning.

"What did you learn?" Mrs. Trump asked.

"Franklin's really good at helping people who are struggling with difficulties that matter to their lives," Donald said. "Not just entertaining people or providing business services, but actually supporting people who need individual attention and authentic care."

Donald described Franklin's consultation work with Michael's social anxiety, the therapeutic support for children with learning differences, and the relationship confidence development that had helped families understand animal care principles and community cooperation concepts.

"Franklin provides genuine therapeutic value," Donald concluded. "And I think he wants to continue using his abilities to help people in our own neighbourhood who might need the kind of individual support that he's naturally good at providing."

Fred Trump set down his newspaper and looked at Donald with obvious pride. "Son, it sounds like you've learned something important about the difference between making money and making a difference."

"Franklin taught me that authentic success comes from actually helping people rather than just beating competition or generating profit," Donald replied. "And I think that's what I want to focus on for the rest of the summer."

Mrs. Trump smiled at her son with the warmth that came from recognizing genuine personal growth. "Donald, we're proud of how you've learned to work with Franklin as a genuine partner rather than just using his abilities for your own advantage."

"What would you like to do about community service consultation?" Fred Trump asked.

Donald felt the kind of confidence that came from understanding meaningful work rather than just ambitious planning.

"I'd like to work with Mrs. Chen and other neighbourhood parents to create consultation opportunities for families who could benefit from Franklin's individual attention and therapeutic support," Donald said. "Not as a business venture, but as genuine community service that helps people with difficulties that are important to their lives."

His parents exchanged looks that Donald recognized as approval and support for authentic community service development.

"That sounds like exactly the kind of summer activity that builds genuine community relationships," Mrs. Trump said.

"And teaches important lessons about service and cooperation," Fred Trump added.

As Donald settled Franklin in his pen that evening, he felt the kind of confidence that came from understanding authentic success and meaningful community contribution.

"Franklin," Donald said, "I think we finally figured out what we're actually supposed to be doing with your abilities and my organizational skills."

Franklin honked thoughtful agreement and performed his sitting trick.

"Helping people who need individual support and authentic attention," Donald continued. "Not because it's profitable or competitive, but because it's the right thing to do and because you're naturally good at providing exactly the kind of care that makes people feel valued and supported."

Franklin gently nudged Donald's hand and honked what sounded like satisfaction with Donald's evolving understanding of genuine service priorities.

As Donald planned community consultation services that would focus on authentic therapeutic support rather than entertainment programming, he felt the kind of confidence that came from understanding meaningful work.

The summer was entering its final phase, but Donald finally understood what Franklin had been trying to teach him about the difference between competitive achievement and authentic friendship.

Franklin honked goodnight, and Donald fell asleep planning consultation services that would help neighbours with real difficulties rather than just providing entertainment for summer recreation.

He still had no idea that the most important test of authentic friendship was waiting just around the corner.

Summer's End Summit

The last week of August arrived with the kind of bittersweet recognition that comes when something important is ending but ending well. Donald's consultation partnership with Franklin had evolved into genuine community service that was requested by families throughout the neighbourhood, and their collaboration with the Feinberg twins had created what Mrs. Chen called "the most constructive summer programming our community has ever seen."

But Tuesday morning brought news that would test everything Donald and Franklin had learned about authentic friendship and meaningful service.

"The Kowalski family is moving," Eddie reported during Tuesday's planning session, his voice carrying the kind of concern that came from understanding genuine loss. "Tommy's dad got transferred to California. They're leaving this weekend."

Donald felt immediate recognition of the challenge this represented. The Kowalski twins had been part of every business venture, party, and community service activity since the garage sale in June. Tommy especially had formed a genuine friendship with Franklin that extended beyond consultation services into authentic personal connection.

"Tommy doesn't know yet," Frankie added quietly. "His parents are planning to tell him tonight. They asked if Franklin might be able to provide consultation support for helping Tommy understand the move and feel confident about making new friends."

Donald looked at Franklin, who was listening to the conversation with obvious concern and occasionally honking what sounded like questions about Tommy's situation.

"This isn't entertainment consultation," Donald realized. "This is helping someone we actually care about deal with one of the most difficult things that happens to kids."

Franklin honked seriously and performed his sitting trick, apparently understanding the importance of the support they were being asked to provide.

"Franklin," Donald said, "Tommy's going to need the best consultation you've ever provided. Not for business reasons or community service reputation, but because he's our friend and he's going to be scared and sad about leaving everything he knows."

Franklin approached Donald and gently nudged his hand, apparently offering reassurance about his commitment to providing genuine therapeutic support for Tommy's transition difficulties.

Tuesday evening's consultation session with Tommy was the most challenging and meaningful service Franklin had provided all summer.

Tommy arrived at Donald's house with his parents, clearly aware that something important was happening but not yet understanding the full scope of his family's transition plans. When his parents explained that the family would be moving to California because of his father's job transfer, Tommy's reaction was immediate and heartbreaking.

"I don't want to move," Tommy said, beginning to cry. "I don't want to leave Franklin and Donald and everyone I know."

Franklin immediately approached Tommy and positioned himself where Tommy could lean against him for physical comfort while processing the emotional complexity of unexpected life changes.

"Franklin's here to help you understand moving," Donald said gently. "He knows that leaving friends is scary and sad, but he also knows that you're brave enough to handle new situations."

Franklin honked softly and remained perfectly still while Tommy cried against his side, providing the kind of patient physical presence that offered comfort without trying to minimize Tommy's legitimate emotional response to difficult news.

"Moving is really hard," Donald continued, sitting down next to Tommy and Franklin. "It's okay to be sad about leaving people you care about. Franklin understands that missing friends is part of caring about them."

Franklin's consultation approach for Tommy was different from any therapeutic support Donald had observed before. Instead of trying to solve Tommy's emotional distress or provide strategic advice about handling transitions, Franklin simply offered authentic presence that allowed Tommy to express his feelings without judgment or pressure to feel better quickly.

"Franklin," Tommy said after several minutes of crying, "will you remember me when I'm in California?"

Franklin honked what could only be interpreted as absolute confirmation and performed his sitting trick specifically for Tommy, clearly communicating that their friendship was genuine and permanent regardless of geographical distance.

"Franklin's friendship doesn't depend on being in the same place," Donald said, understanding something important about authentic relationship commitment. "Real friends care about each other even when they can't be together every day."

The consultation session continued for two hours, with Franklin providing patient support while Tommy processed his feelings about moving and Donald offered strategic consultation about maintaining friendships across distance and building confidence about new social situations.

"Franklin's teaching me that I can be brave even when I'm scared," Tommy said as the session concluded. "And that missing people is okay because it means you care about them."

Donald felt the kind of satisfaction that came from providing genuine therapeutic support rather than just entertainment or business services.

"Tommy," Donald said, "Franklin wants you to know that moving to California means you'll get to make new friends while still keeping the old friends who care about you. You're not losing Franklin's friendship, you're expanding your friend community."

Wednesday and Thursday were spent in intensive preparation for what Donald and Franklin recognized as the most important consultation services of their summer: helping Tommy develop confidence and practical strategies for his family's transition while also creating meaningful conclusion experiences for their own neighbourhood relationships.

"This is genuine therapeutic consultation," Donald told his parents during Wednesday evening's planning briefing. "Tommy needs real support for authentic difficulties, not just entertainment or distraction."

Franklin had apparently understood the importance of Tommy's consultation needs because he was approaching the preparation with unusual seriousness and focus. Instead of his normal playful energy, Franklin was demonstrating the kind of professional attention that suggested genuine commitment to providing effective therapeutic support.

"Franklin's preparing to provide the best consultation he's capable of," Donald observed during Thursday morning's training session. "He understands that Tommy's counting on him for real help with problems that actually matter."

Thursday afternoon brought an unexpected development that would provide the perfect conclusion for both Tommy's transition support and Donald's summer of learning about authentic community service.

Mrs. Henderson approached Donald while he and Franklin were conducting final preparation for Tommy's departure consultation.

"Donald," Mrs. Henderson said, and her tone carried the warmth that had developed since Donald's strategic shift toward genuine community service, "I have a request that might interest you and Franklin."

Donald felt cautious curiosity. Mrs. Henderson's requests had historically resulted in significant complications for Trump family activities.

"The neighbourhood parents have been discussing Tommy's move," Mrs. Henderson continued, "and we wondered if you and Franklin might be willing to coordinate a farewell celebration that would help Tommy feel appreciated and supported while also giving everyone a chance to demonstrate their care for his family."

Donald felt immediate recognition of the opportunity this represented for meaningful community service rather than competitive entertainment programming.

"What kind of farewell celebration?" Donald asked.

"Something that reflects the community relationships Tommy has built this summer," Mrs. Henderson explained. "Personal attention and individual appreciation rather than standard party programming. We thought Franklin's consultation abilities might help coordinate celebration activities that would make Tommy feel genuinely valued and confident about his transition."

Donald looked at Franklin, who was listening to the conversation with obvious interest and occasionally honking what sounded like enthusiasm for community service opportunities.

"Franklin would be honoured to provide consultation services for Tommy's farewell celebration," Donald said. "We'll work with the twins to create community programming that focuses on authentic appreciation and genuine support for Tommy's transition."

Friday's collaborative planning for Tommy's farewell celebration demonstrated that Donald's summer of learning about cooperation and authentic service had prepared him for community coordination that exceeded any of his previous organizational achievements.

The twins contributed their systematic organizational capabilities to create efficient celebration logistics and community coordination. Donald and Franklin focused on personalized consultation that would ensure Tommy received individual attention and authentic appreciation from everyone who cared about him.

"This is community service coordination at its most meaningful," Madeline observed during Friday afternoon's planning session.

"Genuine therapeutic support combined with systematic celebration organization," Josephine added.

Franklin honked agreement and performed his sitting trick for the collaborative planning team, apparently satisfied with the community service strategic direction.

"The goal," Donald said, "is to help Tommy understand that he's genuinely valued by this community and that moving to California doesn't mean losing the friendships he's built here."

Friday evening's final preparation included Donald's most important strategic conversation of the entire summer: a private consultation session with Franklin about their own partnership and what they'd learned about authentic friendship through their community service experiences.

"Franklin," Donald said, sitting in the backyard after completing celebration planning, "this summer you've taught me things about friendship and service that I never understood from business magazines or competitive strategies."

Franklin honked thoughtfully and approached Donald for close consultation positioning.

"You've shown me that authentic success comes from helping people with problems that actually matter to their lives," Donald continued. "Not just entertaining them or impressing them or beating competition, but actually providing support that makes their situations better."

Franklin performed his sitting trick and looked at Donald with patient attention.

"And I think," Donald said, "maybe the most important thing you've taught me is that real friendship means caring about what's good for the other person, not just what's good for yourself."

Franklin gently nudged Donald's hand and honked what sounded like confirmation and appreciation for Donald's evolving understanding of authentic relationship principles.

Saturday morning's farewell celebration for Tommy began with what Donald immediately recognized as the most meaningful community service event of his summer.

The entire neighbourhood had gathered in the park to demonstrate their appreciation for Tommy and their support for his family's transition. But instead of standard farewell party programming, Franklin was providing individualized consultation that helped Tommy understand the genuine impact he'd had on his community and the authentic friendships he'd developed.

"Tommy," Donald said as Franklin positioned himself for individual consultation, "everyone here wants you to know that you've been an important part of our community and that moving to California doesn't change how much people care about you."

Franklin honked agreement and began what appeared to be comprehensive consultation about friendship permanence, transition confidence, and the difference between geographical distance and authentic relationship commitment.

Franklin's consultation approach for Tommy demonstrated the full scope of therapeutic abilities he'd developed throughout the summer. He provided patient attention while Tommy expressed his feelings about leaving, offered physical comfort when Tommy needed reassurance, and demonstrated through his own authentic care that genuine friendships survive geographical separation.

"Franklin's showing me that real friends don't forget each other just because they live in different places," Tommy said during the consultation session.

"Franklin's also showing you that you're capable of making new friends while keeping the old friends who care about you," Donald added, providing strategic consultation that reflected everything Franklin had taught him about confidence development and relationship building.

The celebration continued for three hours, with Franklin providing individual consultation to Tommy while the broader community demonstrated their appreciation through organized activities, shared memories, and genuine expressions of care that exceeded anything Donald had witnessed during his summer of entertainment programming.

"This is real community service," Lisa told Donald as they watched Franklin help Tommy understand that moving was an adventure rather than just a loss. "Franklin's helping Tommy feel confident about his future while also showing him how much his current community cares about him."

Donald felt the kind of satisfaction that came from facilitating authentic therapeutic support rather than competitive entertainment programming.

"Franklin's taught me that the best way to help someone who's facing difficulties is to provide genuine care and authentic attention," Donald replied. "Not trying to fix their problems or distract them from difficulties, but helping them understand their own capabilities and the authentic support that's available from people who care about them."

The celebration's emotional highlight came when Tommy specifically requested private consultation time with Franklin for what he called "important friendship conversation."

Donald watched Tommy and Franklin settle into quiet consultation positioning while the broader celebration continued around them. Franklin listened attentively while Tommy talked, honked thoughtful responses, and provided the kind of individual attention that clearly made Tommy feel valued and supported during one of the most difficult transitions of his young life.

"What are they talking about?" Eddie asked.

"I don't know," Donald replied. "But Franklin's providing exactly the kind of authentic consultation that Tommy needs, and that's what matters."

Donald realized that Franklin's consultation with Tommy represented the culmination of everything they'd learned about genuine service and authentic friendship throughout the summer. Franklin was providing therapeutic support that adapted to Tommy's individual needs while demonstrating the kind of authentic care that created genuine confidence and relationship security.

The celebration concluded with what everyone agreed was the most meaningful community service event the neighbourhood had experienced all year. Tommy was clearly feeling more confident about his family's transition, the community had demonstrated genuine appreciation for the Kowalski family's contributions, and Franklin had provided therapeutic consultation that helped everyone understand the permanence of authentic friendship despite geographical changes.

"Thank you," Mr. Kowalski told Donald as the celebration wound down and families began preparing for the Kowalski family's departure the following morning. "Franklin provided exactly the kind of support that Tommy needed to feel confident about our move. You should be proud of what you've both accomplished this summer."

Donald felt the kind of recognition that came from community appreciation for genuine service rather than competitive business achievement.

"Franklin taught me that authentic success comes from actually helping people rather than just impressing them," Donald replied. "Tommy's friendship has been important to both of us, and we wanted to make sure he felt supported during this transition."

Sunday morning's departure of the Kowalski family marked the end of Donald's summer of learning about business, competition, and community service, but it also marked the beginning of his understanding of authentic friendship and meaningful life priorities.

Donald and Franklin were present when the moving truck arrived to collect the Kowalski family's belongings. Tommy approached Franklin for final consultation about transition confidence and friendship permanence.

"Franklin," Tommy said, hugging the pig while trying not to cry again, "will you teach other kids the things you taught me?"

Franklin honked what could only be interpreted as solemn commitment and performed his sitting trick specifically for Tommy, clearly communicating his dedication to continuing the kind of therapeutic consultation that had helped Tommy develop confidence and relationship understanding.

"Franklin will continue providing consultation services for children who need individual attention and authentic support," Donald promised. "Your friendship taught both of us important things about caring for people who are facing difficulties."

As the Kowalski family's car pulled away from the neighbourhood, Donald felt the kind of meaningful sadness that came from genuine friendship transitions rather than just entertainment relationship conclusions.

"Franklin," Donald said, sitting next to his pig while they watched Tommy wave goodbye from the car window, "this summer we learned that the most important business we can be in is the friendship business."

Franklin honked thoughtful agreement and leaned against Donald, apparently understanding that meaningful endings required emotional processing and mutual support.

Sunday afternoon's reflection on the summer's experiences brought Donald to final recognition of what Franklin had been teaching him about authentic success and genuine community contribution.

"Franklin," Donald said during their concluding consultation session, "when I started this summer, I thought success meant beating other people and making the most money and creating the biggest business ventures."

Franklin honked patiently and looked at Donald with the kind of attention that encouraged continued strategic thinking.

"But you showed me that real success means helping people who need support and providing authentic service that actually matters to their lives," Donald continued. "And that genuine friendship is more valuable than any competitive advantage or profit margin."

Franklin performed his sitting trick and honked what sounded like pride in Donald's evolving understanding of meaningful priorities.

"The best business we ever created," Donald said, "was learning to be genuine friends who help people with problems that are important to them."

Franklin gently nudged Donald's hand and honked agreement, apparently satisfied with Donald's summer-long learning about authentic relationship principles and community service priorities.

As Donald settled Franklin in his pen for what felt like the conclusion of their intensive summer partnership, he felt the kind of confidence that came from understanding meaningful work and authentic success.

"Next week school starts," Donald told Franklin. "But the consultation services we've developed and the community relationships we've built, those continue because they're based on genuine care rather than just summer entertainment."

Franklin honked thoughtful agreement and looked toward the fence that separated them from the neighbourhood, but not with ambitious energy for new business ventures. Instead, Franklin seemed to be considering ongoing service opportunities that would continue helping people throughout the year.

Monday morning brought the final validation of Donald's summer learning when Mrs. Chen called with a request that demonstrated the permanent impact of Franklin's consultation services and Donald's evolution toward authentic community contribution.

"Donald," Mrs. Chen said, "several neighbourhood parents have been discussing Franklin's therapeutic consultation abilities and your organizational coordination skills. We wondered if you might be interested in continuing community service programming throughout the school year."

Donald felt the kind of recognition that came from community appreciation for genuine service rather than temporary summer entertainment.

"What kind of community service programming?" Donald asked.

"Ongoing consultation support for families who could benefit from Franklin's individual attention and your collaborative coordination," Mrs. Chen explained. "Therapeutic assistance for children who are struggling with school transitions, social difficulties, or confidence development. We've seen how effective Franklin's consultation approach is for children who need personalized support."

Donald looked at Franklin, who was listening to the conversation with obvious interest and occasionally honking what sounded like enthusiasm for expanded community service opportunities.

"Franklin and I would be honoured to continue providing consultation services for families who need individual attention and therapeutic support," Donald said. "Not as a business venture, but as ongoing community service that helps people with difficulties that are important to their lives."

Monday afternoon's final planning session with Eddie, Frankie, and the Feinberg twins brought Donald to complete understanding of what he and Franklin had accomplished during their summer of learning about authentic partnership and meaningful community contribution.

"We started the summer trying to build profitable business ventures that would beat the competition," Donald told the collaborative planning team. "But we ended up learning that the most important work involves helping people who need genuine support and authentic attention."

Madeline and Josephine exchanged glances that suggested they were recognizing Donald's authentic strategic evolution rather than competitive repositioning.

"Franklin's consultation abilities provide therapeutic value that extends beyond entertainment into genuine community service," Madeline observed.

"Donald's organizational coordination creates service opportunities that connect Franklin's abilities with families who need individual attention," Josephine added.

Franklin honked agreement and performed his sitting trick for the entire collaborative team, apparently satisfied with the community service strategic direction they'd developed through their summer of learning about cooperation rather than competition.

"What we learned," Donald continued, "is that authentic success comes from using your actual abilities to help people with problems that genuinely matter to their lives. Not trying to prove you're better than other people, but working together to provide service that makes people's situations actually better."

The planning session concluded with commitments from everyone to continue collaborative community service throughout the school year, focusing on therapeutic consultation, educational support, and authentic attention for families who could benefit from individualized care and genuine relationship building.

"Franklin's Individual Consultation Services," Donald announced as they concluded Monday's final planning session. "Continuing throughout the year because genuine community service doesn't end when summer ends."

Franklin honked official approval and performed his sitting trick for all his human partners.

Monday evening's conversation with his parents about the summer's learning and future community service commitments brought Donald to the most important strategic recognition of his entire experience.

"Mom, Dad," Donald said, joining his parents in the living room for what felt like the most serious business conversation of his life, "I want to talk about what Franklin and I learned this summer and how we want to continue serving our community."

Fred and Mary Trump looked at their son with obvious pride and attention.

"Franklin taught me that the most important business success comes from actually helping people rather than just making money or beating competition," Donald said. "And I think that's what I want to focus on for the rest of my life."

Donald described Franklin's therapeutic consultation work, the collaborative partnerships they'd developed, and the genuine community service that had grown from their summer of learning about authentic relationship building and meaningful contribution.

"Franklin's abilities are valuable because he provides individual attention and authentic care that helps people with difficulties that are important to their lives," Donald concluded. "And I think my abilities are valuable when I use them to facilitate Franklin's consultation services and coordinate community service that actually makes people's situations better."

Fred Trump set down his newspaper and looked at Donald with obvious respect. "Son, you've learned something this summer that many adults never understand. That genuine success comes from service rather than competition, and that authentic relationships are more valuable than business achievements."

"Franklin's been an excellent teacher," Mrs. Trump added. "And you've been an excellent student of friendship and community responsibility."

Donald felt the kind of recognition that came from parental approval for personal growth rather than just summer activity management.

"What Franklin and I want to do," Donald said, "is continue providing consultation services for families who need individual therapeutic support, educational assistance, and authentic attention. Not because it's profitable, but because it's meaningful work that uses our actual abilities to help people with genuine needs."

His parents exchanged looks that Donald recognized as complete support for authentic community service development.

"That sounds like exactly the kind of life purpose that builds genuine community relationships and personal satisfaction," Fred Trump said.

"And teaches important lessons about service, cooperation, and authentic success," Mrs. Trump added.

As Donald settled Franklin in his pen for the final time as a summer business partner and for the first time as a genuine friend and community service collaborator, he felt the kind of confidence that came from understanding meaningful work and authentic relationship priorities.

"Franklin," Donald said, "this summer you taught me that the best business we could ever create is genuine friendship and authentic service to people who need support."

Franklin honked thoughtful agreement and performed his sitting trick.

"And I learned," Donald continued, "that real success doesn't come from beating other people or making the most money. It comes from using your abilities to help people with problems that actually matter to their lives."

Franklin gently nudged Donald's hand and honked what sounded like satisfaction with Donald's complete understanding of authentic service priorities and meaningful relationship principles.

As Donald planned ongoing consultation services that would focus on genuine therapeutic support rather than entertainment programming, he felt the kind of confidence that came from understanding his life's purpose.

The summer of 1962 had ended, but Donald's education in authentic friendship and meaningful community service was just beginning.

Franklin honked goodnight, and Donald fell asleep planning consultation services that would help neighbours throughout the year rather than just providing entertainment for summer recreation.

School would start Tuesday, but Donald finally understood that the most important learning happened through authentic relationships and genuine service to people who needed support.

And Franklin, Franklin would continue being exactly what he'd always been: the best friend and wisest teacher Donald had ever had the privilege of knowing.

The Trump Family Halloween Special

October had arrived with the kind of crisp autumn air that made Donald Trump feel like reinventing himself was not only possible but inevitable. School had started three weeks earlier, which meant his summer of community service consultation with Franklin had been replaced by homework, pop quizzes, and the grinding social hierarchy of Jamaica High School, where being known as "the kid with the business pig" was not necessarily the reputation Donald had hoped to cultivate.

But salvation arrived on a Thursday afternoon in the form of an engraved invitation that would either represent Donald's social comeback or his final descent into family legend infamy. "Donald," his mother called from the kitchen, holding what appeared to be expensive stationery with the kind of formal lettering that suggested serious social importance. "Your Aunt Millicent has invited our family to spend Halloween weekend at the Vanderbilt estate."

Donald felt immediate recognition of the opportunity this represented. The Vanderbilt cousins were sophisticated, wealthy, and most importantly, completely unaware of Donald's summer reputation for pig-related community disruption. This was his chance to demonstrate mature business acumen and social capability without the baggage of neighbourhood notoriety.

"The Hudson Valley estate?" Donald asked, trying to project casual interest rather than desperate social ambition.

"The haunted mansion," his father added with obvious amusement. "Aunt Millicent's annual Halloween extravaganza for the family's teenage contingent. Three days of sophisticated entertainment and what she calls 'age-appropriate social development opportunities.'" Donald's mind immediately began calculating strategic possibilities. Sophisticated relatives, mature social environment, and complete absence of anyone who remembered the garage sale incident or the Fourth of July Revolutionary War reenactment. This was exactly the kind of premium networking opportunity that successful businessmen leveraged for long-term relationship development. "I'll pack my best suit," Donald announced.

What Donald didn't announce was his private strategic assessment that Franklin's consultation abilities could provide significant competitive advantage in an environment where he needed to establish credibility with sophisticated relatives who appreciated intelligence and strategic thinking.

Friday evening's packing session included what Donald called "comprehensive social preparation" and what would later be remembered as the most creatively ambitious transportation logistics of his fifteen-year career.

"Franklin," Donald said quietly as he prepared his father's largest suitcase, "this weekend represents a crucial opportunity for our partnership to demonstrate sophistication and strategic intelligence in an elevated social environment."

Franklin honked thoughtfully and looked at the suitcase with obvious interest.

"The thing is," Donald continued, "Aunt Millicent specifically requested 'no farm animals at the estate.' But she doesn't understand your consultation abilities or your social intelligence. She's thinking about regular pigs, not strategic business partners."

Franklin performed his sitting trick and honked what sounded like understanding of the diplomatic challenge involved.

"So, we need to approach this situation with creative logistics," Donald said, opening the suitcase and examining its internal dimensions. "Temporary transportation concealment until we can demonstrate your strategic value to the assembled family members."

Franklin approached the suitcase and conducted what appeared to be professional assessment of its accommodation possibilities. After several minutes of systematic investigation, Franklin honked what Donald interpreted as qualified approval of the transportation plan.

"Just until we get there," Donald promised. "Once they see your consultation abilities, they'll understand that you're a strategic asset, not a farm animal."

Franklin's willingness to participate in concealed transportation logistics demonstrated either complete trust in Donald's social planning or pig-level understanding of the importance of weekend getaway opportunities.

The drive to the Hudson Valley passed uneventfully, with Franklin maintaining professional silence from within the suitcase while Donald reviewed his strategic objectives for sophisticated relative relationship development.

The Vanderbilt estate was more impressive than Donald had anticipated. Three stories of Victorian gothic architecture, surrounded by grounds that suggested serious family wealth and the kind of social sophistication that Donald associated with genuine business success.

"Donald," Aunt Millicent greeted him as the family arrived, "you've grown tremendously since last Christmas. I understand you've been developing entrepreneurial interests this summer?"

Donald felt immediate validation. Aunt Millicent's recognition of his business development suggested that news of his strategic capabilities had reached sophisticated family circles.
"I've been learning about community service coordination and strategic consultation delivery," Donald replied, using the professional terminology he'd developed during his collaboration with the Feinberg twins.

"How impressive," Aunt Millicent said. "You'll have wonderful opportunities to network with your cousins this weekend. Bradley and Trevor have been developing quite sophisticated social interests lately."

Donald felt confident that his weekend strategy was already generating positive results. Sophisticated cousins with social interests would clearly appreciate consultation about strategic relationship development and business networking approaches.

The first indication that Donald's strategic assessment might require adjustment came when he met his cousins in the estate's main parlour.

Bradley Vanderbilt was sixteen, wore his hair in the kind of deliberately casual style that required significant grooming effort, and was currently engaged in what appeared to be detailed discussion with his fifteen-year-old cousin Trevor about optimal techniques for accessing the estate's wine cellar without parental detection.

"Donald!" Bradley called out when Aunt Millicent introduced the arriving family members. "Great to see you, cousin. We were just discussing weekend recreational planning. You interested in some serious fun?"

Donald felt immediate enthusiasm for sophisticated recreational coordination. "Absolutely. I've developed considerable expertise in entertainment planning and strategic activity coordination."
Bradley and Trevor exchanged glances that Donald interpreted as recognition of his professional capabilities.

"Excellent," Trevor said. "Because we've got some premium entertainment opportunities lined up for tonight. Very exclusive. Very adult. Think you can handle advanced social activities?"
Donald felt the kind of confidence that came from sophisticated relatives recognizing his maturity and strategic thinking abilities. "I've been coordinating advanced programming all summer. Premium entertainment is exactly my area of expertise."

"Perfect," Bradley said. "Meet us in the library at eleven tonight. We'll show you how sophisticated people really have fun."
Donald spent Friday evening unpacking his strategic materials and settling Franklin into temporary concealment within his bedroom's large armoire. The estate bedrooms were spacious enough to accommodate creative pet management, and Franklin seemed comfortable with the upgraded accommodation arrangements.
"Franklin," Donald said quietly as he provided Franklin with snacks and water within the armoire, "tonight we demonstrate sophisticated consultation abilities to relatives who appreciate strategic intelligence and mature social coordination."

Franklin honked softly and performed his sitting trick within the confined space, apparently understanding the importance of maintaining concealment during initial strategic positioning.
At exactly eleven o'clock, Donald arrived at the library wearing his father's best suit and carrying his notebook for documenting sophisticated networking opportunities and advanced social coordination concepts.

What Donald found was Bradley and Trevor engaged in what appeared to be systematic wine theft from a locked cabinet, while discussing optimal strategies for locating private spaces where they could pursue what Trevor diplomatically described as "mature romantic coordination activities."

"Donald!" Bradley called out, holding a bottle of what appeared to be expensive wine. "Perfect timing. We were just conducting inventory assessment of recreational enhancement supplies." Donald felt immediate confusion. "Recreational enhancement supplies?"

"Liquid confidence for advanced social interaction," Trevor explained, opening the wine bottle with practiced efficiency. "Essential equipment for sophisticated teenage social programming."

Donald watched his cousins pour wine into coffee cups and realized that their definition of sophisticated entertainment involved activities that his parents would definitely classify as inappropriate teenage behaviour rather than strategic business networking. "So," Bradley said, offering Donald a cup of wine, "what's your experience with advanced romantic coordination? Trevor and I have been developing quite sophisticated approaches to teenage relationship development."

Donald felt his strategic confidence wavering. "I've been focusing more on business consultation and community service coordination," he said carefully.

"Business consultation?" Trevor looked confused. "Donald, we're talking about making out with girls. You know, the thing normal teenagers spend most of their time thinking about?"

Donald realized that his sophisticated relatives were primarily interested in activities that had nothing to do with strategic thinking, professional development, or business networking. They wanted to drink stolen wine and pursue romantic activities with whatever teenage girls were available for sophisticated social interaction.
"Oh," Donald said. "Romance coordination. I've been... developing expertise in that area too."

This was a complete lie. Donald's romantic coordination experience was limited to awkward conversations with Lisa Chen and strategic anxiety about whether girls appreciated business acumen in potential relationship partners.

"Great," Bradley said, clearly assuming Donald's business focus was just teenage awkwardness about discussing romantic interests. "Because Jessica Morrison and Sarah Patterson are here for the weekend, and they're both very interested in sophisticated social activities with mature teenage guys."

Donald felt panic and excitement simultaneously. Jessica Morrison was sixteen, beautiful, and had never demonstrated any awareness of Donald's existence during their limited interactions at neighbourhood social events. The possibility that she might be interested in sophisticated social activities with him seemed both thrilling and completely implausible.

"What kind of sophisticated activities?" Donald asked.
"Standard teenage party activities," Trevor replied. "Drinking wine, playing games that involve proximity and physical contact, finding dark corners for private conversation and whatever develops naturally from private conversation."

Donald's notebook contained extensive strategic planning for business networking and professional relationship development, but nothing about romantic coordination or sophisticated teenage social activities that involved alcohol and deliberate proximity engineering. "I should mention," Donald said carefully, "I've brought a strategic consultation asset who might enhance our recreational programming this weekend."

"Strategic consultation asset?" Bradley looked intrigued. "What kind of asset?"

Donald felt immediate recognition that Franklin's introduction required diplomatic preparation and sophisticated presentation. "Franklin Roosevelt," Donald said. "Highly intelligent, natural social coordination abilities, proven expertise in group activity facilitation and individual consultation services."

"Franklin Roosevelt?" Trevor looked confused. "You brought a friend named Franklin?"

"Not exactly a friend," Donald replied. "More of a... specialized consultation partner."

Donald was trying to present Franklin's abilities in terms that would appeal to sophisticated relatives without immediately revealing the pig-related aspects of their partnership.

"Consultation partner for what?" Bradley asked.
"Strategic entertainment coordination, social activity optimization, and advanced group psychology management," Donald said, using the professional terminology he'd developed during summer community service programming.

Bradley and Trevor exchanged glances that suggested they were either impressed by Donald's sophisticated consultation capabilities or confused by his business-focused approach to weekend recreational planning.

"Where is this Franklin?" Trevor asked.
"Temporary strategic positioning," Donald replied. "He'll be available for consultation services once I've assessed the optimal introduction timing and social integration protocols."

What Donald meant was that Franklin was concealed in his bedroom armoire until Donald could figure out how to present a pig to sophisticated relatives who were primarily interested in wine theft and romantic coordination activities.

The Friday night "sophisticated entertainment" turned out to be considerably less strategic than Donald had anticipated.
Bradley and Trevor led Donald to the estate's basement, where they'd established what they called their "advanced social coordination headquarters", essentially a collection of stolen wine, comfortable seating, and mood lighting designed to facilitate what Donald gradually understood was standard teenage party behaviour.
"The thing about sophisticated social activities," Bradley explained as they settled into the basement setup, "is that success depends on creating environments where people feel comfortable with physical proximity and emotional vulnerability."

Donald made notes in his strategic planning notebook, though he was beginning to realize that his cousins' approach to social coordination focused more on alcohol-assisted confidence development than on systematic relationship building.
"So, the wine reduces social anxiety and facilitates natural conversation development?" Donald asked, trying to understand romantic coordination through business strategy terminology.
"Exactly," Trevor confirmed. "Plus, it makes everything more fun and creates shared experience bonding between participants."

Donald felt like he was receiving advanced education in social psychology, though the educational methodology seemed to involve more alcohol consumption than he'd expected from sophisticated teenage programming.

The educational session was interrupted at approximately one-thirty in the morning by sounds from the estate's upper floors that could only be described as mysterious, rhythmic, and definitely not explicable through conventional Halloween decoration or standard building maintenance.

Thump. Snort. Thump-thump. SNORT.
"What the hell is that?" Bradley asked, looking toward the basement ceiling with obvious concern.

The sounds continued with increasing volume and what appeared to be systematic movement throughout the estate's upper floors. THUMP. Snort-snort-snort. CRASH.

"That sounds like someone, or something, is moving around upstairs," Trevor observed, setting down his wine cup with the sudden sobriety that comes with potential security concerns.
Donald felt immediate panic. The sounds were unmistakably Franklin-related, which meant his strategic consultation partner had somehow escaped from armoire concealment and was conducting independent exploration of estate facilities.

"Maybe it's just house settling," Donald suggested desperately. "Old buildings make unusual sounds, especially on Halloween weekend."
SNORT-SNORT-SNORT. Crash. Tinkle of breaking glass.
"Houses don't snort," Bradley pointed out.
From the floors above came the unmistakable sound of adult voices expressing alarm and confusion about mysterious nocturnal activities.

"THERE'S SOMETHING IN THE WALLS!" Aunt Millicent's voice carried clearly through the estate's vintage architecture. "THE GHOST OF GREAT-UNCLE MORTIMER HAS RETURNED!" Uncle Reginald's voice suggested that sophisticated adults were developing supernatural explanations for mysterious nighttime disturbances.

Donald realized that Franklin's independent estate exploration was generating exactly the kind of family attention that would compromise his strategic social positioning objectives.
"We should probably investigate," Donald said, trying to project helpful concern rather than guilty knowledge about the source of mysterious estate disturbances.

"Definitely," Bradley agreed. "Sophisticated teenagers take initiative during potential security situations."

Donald followed his cousins upstairs while frantically developing strategic plans for Franklin location, retrieval, and damage control that would preserve his weekend networking opportunities.
The estate's main floor was in controlled chaos, with Aunt Millicent, Uncle Reginald, and Donald's parents conducting systematic investigation of mysterious sound sources while developing increasingly elaborate supernatural explanations for unusual nocturnal activities.

"It started in the east wing," Aunt Millicent reported to the assembled family members. "Rhythmic thumping, followed by what sounded like... breathing. Heavy breathing. From something large."
"Large breathing something that moves through the walls," Uncle Reginald added. "Great-Uncle Mortimer was a substantial man. His spiritual presence would naturally generate significant acoustic phenomena."

Donald listened to his sophisticated relatives develop ghost theories for Franklin's exploration activities and realized that his consultation partner's strategic reconnaissance had inadvertently created the most entertaining Halloween programming the estate had experienced in decades.

"Maybe we should check the individual rooms?" Donald suggested, hoping to locate Franklin before his exploration activities generated additional supernatural evidence.

"Excellent idea," Aunt Millicent agreed. "Systematic investigation will either confirm supernatural presence or identify conventional explanations for unusual estate phenomena."

The family divided into search teams and began methodical room-by-room investigation while Franklin apparently continued his comprehensive estate consultation from some undetermined location within the building's extensive floor plan.

Donald was assigned to search the library with Bradley and Trevor, which meant he couldn't conduct private Franklin location activities without arousing sophisticated cousin suspicion about his mysterious familiarity with estate disturbance patterns.
"Donald," Bradley said as they searched the library for ghost evidence, "you seem unusually knowledgeable about mysterious sound investigation procedures."

"Strategic thinking," Donald replied, though his strategic thinking was focused entirely on Franklin retrieval rather than supernatural phenomenon analysis.

The library search was interrupted by renewed mysterious activities from what appeared to be the estate's kitchen area.
SNORT. Crash. Tinkle-tinkle-crash. SNORT-SNORT.

"The kitchen," Trevor said. "Something's definitely in the kitchen." Donald felt immediate recognition that Franklin had discovered estate food service facilities and was conducting the kind of systematic investigation that had characterized his approach to neighbourhood customer consultation throughout the summer. "Should we investigate?" Bradley asked.

"Sophisticated teenagers coordinate with adult supervision during potential security situations," Donald said desperately, hoping to delay Franklin discovery until he could develop appropriate damage control strategies.

But Bradley and Trevor were clearly excited by the prospect of direct ghost encounter opportunities, and they headed toward the kitchen with the enthusiasm of people who'd been drinking wine and were therefore convinced of their ability to handle supernatural phenomena.

Donald followed his cousins toward the kitchen while developing emergency strategic plans for Franklin situation management that would preserve both his consultation partner's safety and his own weekend networking objectives.

The kitchen investigation revealed evidence of Franklin's systematic exploration but no actual Franklin. Cabinet doors were open, food containers had been investigated, and the floor showed what could generously be described as "muddy paw prints" but which Donald recognized as unmistakable pig hoof evidence.

"Look at this," Bradley said, examining the muddy prints with obvious fascination. "These aren't human footprints. They're... something else."

"Something with hooves," Trevor added. "But what kind of ghost has hooves?"

Donald felt desperate inspiration. "Great-Uncle Mortimer was known for his... unusual pets," he said, improvising supernatural family history. "Maybe his spiritual presence includes his favourite animals?"

This explanation seemed to satisfy his cousins' supernatural curiosity while providing cover for Franklin's investigation evidence. "Ghost pets," Bradley said with obvious excitement. "That's way cooler than just regular human ghosts."

The kitchen investigation was interrupted by renewed mysterious activities from what appeared to be the estate's upper floors, followed by adult voices expressing escalating concern about supernatural phenomena and the possibility that the estate was experiencing more extensive haunting than usual.
"Boys!" Aunt Millicent called from the main hallway. "Please return to the parlour! We're coordinating comprehensive supernatural investigation protocols!"

Donald followed his cousins back to the parlour while privately calculating that Franklin's estate exploration was generating family entertainment that exceeded anything Aunt Millicent had planned for Halloween weekend programming.
Saturday morning brought confirmation that Franklin's nocturnal exploration activities had established him as the estate's primary supernatural phenomenon, with family members developing increasingly elaborate theories about Great-Uncle Mortimer's spiritual presence and his apparent commitment to comprehensive estate haunting.

"The phenomena are definitely increasing in frequency and complexity," Uncle Reginald reported during Saturday breakfast, consulting notes he'd apparently been taking about mysterious estate activities. "Last night's kitchen investigation, followed by what appeared to be systematic exploration of the second-floor guest rooms."

Donald felt both pride in Franklin's thorough consultation approach and panic about the escalating supernatural attention his consultation partner was generating.

"What kind of exploration?" Donald asked, trying to assess the scope of Franklin's independent estate activities.

"Methodical investigation of each room," Aunt Millicent replied. "Great-Uncle Mortimer appears to be conducting comprehensive spiritual inventory of estate facilities. Very thorough. Very systematic."

Donald recognized Franklin's characteristic approach to strategic consultation and realized that his pig was providing systematic estate analysis while adults interpreted his professional thoroughness as supernatural phenomena.

"Maybe Great-Uncle Mortimer is ensuring that estate facilities meet appropriate supernatural standards?" Donald suggested, trying to present Franklin's activities as helpful rather than disruptive. "Excellent theory," Uncle Reginald agreed. "Spiritual quality control for optimal haunting effectiveness."

Saturday afternoon's planned activities included what Aunt Millicent called "sophisticated teenage entertainment coordination", which turned out to be her diplomatic term for providing wine-accessible

spaces where older teenage cousins could pursue romantic activities while adults maintained plausible supervision denial.
"The estate has many private areas suitable for mature teenage social exploration," Aunt Millicent explained to the assembled family members. "Supervised independence that allows young people to develop appropriate social skills."

Donald felt immediate recognition that sophisticated family Halloween programming included systematic facilitation of romantic coordination activities that his parents would definitely classify as inappropriately advanced for fifteen-year-old social development. "Bradley and Trevor will coordinate teenage activity programming," Aunt Millicent continued. "Donald, you're welcome to participate in whatever social activities match your comfort level and maturity preferences."

Donald felt the kind of social pressure that came from sophisticated relatives expecting him to demonstrate appropriate teenage interest in romantic coordination rather than business networking and strategic consultation.

"I'm definitely interested in advanced social activities," Donald said, though he had no idea what advanced social activities actually involved beyond wine consumption and proximity engineering. Saturday afternoon's sophisticated teenage programming took place in the estate's conservatory, where Bradley and Trevor had established what they called "optimal social interaction environment", dim lighting, comfortable seating arrangements, and background music designed to facilitate conversation and whatever developed naturally from conversation.

The other weekend participants included Jessica Morrison and Sarah Patterson, both sixteen and both demonstrating social sophistication that made Donald's business-focused conversation approaches seem distinctly amateur by comparison.

"Donald," Jessica said as the afternoon social activities began, "Bradley mentioned that you've been developing strategic consultation capabilities. That sounds very mature."
Donald felt immediate validation that his business expertise was generating sophisticated female attention and social recognition. "I've been learning about strategic planning, organizational coordination, and consultation delivery that provides genuine value for people who need individualized support," Donald replied, falling into his professional consultation terminology.

"That's fascinating," Sarah said. "What kind of consultation do you provide?"

Donald felt the opportunity to demonstrate his strategic thinking abilities and professional development to sophisticated teenage audiences who would appreciate business acumen and organizational intelligence.

"Comprehensive problem-solving consultation, strategic activity coordination, and customized support delivery that adapts to individual client needs and preferences," Donald said, consulting his notebook for optimal terminology.

Jessica and Sarah exchanged glances that Donald hoped indicated impressed recognition of his consultation capabilities.
"Donald," Bradley said quietly, "maybe we could focus on more standard teenage conversation topics? You know, music, movies, school, social activities that don't require strategic planning?"
Donald felt immediate confusion. "But strategic planning is what creates successful social activities and optimal entertainment coordination."

"Donald," Trevor said patiently, "we're trying to create romantic atmosphere, not business consultation environment. Girls appreciate guys who can talk about normal teenage things, not strategic optimization protocols."

Donald looked at Jessica and Sarah, who were clearly waiting for him to demonstrate normal teenage conversation abilities rather than professional consultation expertise.

"Right," Donald said uncertainly. "Normal teenage conversation. Music and... movies and... social activities."

This should have been straightforward, but Donald discovered that his summer of business focus and strategic planning had not prepared him for casual conversation about topics that didn't involve organizational objectives or consultation service delivery. "What kind of music do you like?" Jessica asked, apparently attempting to facilitate normal teenage social interaction.

Donald's mind went blank. His music listening experience consisted primarily of background audio during strategic planning sessions and whatever played on the radio during Franklin consultation activities. "Professional music," Donald said finally. "Strategic listening that enhances concentration during business planning activities." Jessica and Sarah exchanged glances that suggested Donald's conversation approach was not generating the sophisticated social interaction his cousins had anticipated.

"Donald," Sarah said gently, "do you maybe want to just... talk about regular teenage things? Like what you do for fun when you're not working on business projects?"

Donald felt immediate panic. His summer activities had been entirely focused on business ventures, competitive positioning, and community service consultation. He didn't have regular teenage fun activities that didn't involve strategic planning or Franklin's consultation services.

"Fun activities," Donald repeated, trying to identify recreational experiences that didn't require organizational coordination or profit margin calculations.

The sophisticated social interaction was further complicated by the return of mysterious estate phenomena, which interrupted romantic atmosphere development with supernatural entertainment that clearly fascinated everyone more than Donald's strategic conversation approaches.

Thump-thump-snort. CRASH.

"There it is again," Bradley said, looking toward the conservatory ceiling with obvious excitement.

"Great-Uncle Mortimer's spiritual presence," Sarah added. "I've never experienced authentic supernatural phenomena before." Donald felt immediate recognition that Franklin's estate exploration was generating more social interest than his strategic consultation expertise, which meant his consultation partner was inadvertently dominating sophisticated weekend programming.

"Maybe we should investigate the supernatural phenomena?" Donald suggested, hoping to redirect social attention toward Franklin location and retrieval activities.

"Great idea," Jessica agreed. "Sophisticated teenagers coordinate direct supernatural investigation rather than just listening to mysterious sounds."

Donald followed his cousins and their sophisticated female companions toward the source of Franklin's exploration activities while developing emergency damage control strategies that would preserve both Franklin's safety and his own weekend social objectives.

The investigation led to the estate's main staircase, where the mysterious phenomena were clearly originating from the second-floor area and moving systematically between rooms with the thoroughness that Donald recognized as Franklin's characteristic consultation approach.

"It's conducting room-by-room investigation," Trevor observed, listening to the systematic movement patterns with obvious admiration.

"Very organized ghost," Bradley added. "Great-Uncle Mortimer's spiritual presence demonstrates impressive strategic thinking." Donald felt pride in Franklin's systematic exploration abilities and panic about the increasing supernatural attention his consultation partner was generating among family members and sophisticated teenage guests.

"Maybe we should coordinate with adult supervision before conducting direct supernatural investigation?" Donald suggested, hoping to delay Franklin discovery until he could develop appropriate introduction strategies.

"Adults don't understand teenage supernatural investigation capabilities," Jessica replied. "We're more open to authentic spiritual phenomena than parents who focus on conventional explanations." This was exactly the kind of sophisticated teenage reasoning that Donald recognized as potentially problematic for Franklin concealment and damage control objectives.

The supernatural investigation continued to the second floor, where Franklin's systematic exploration had apparently progressed to what sounded like comprehensive room-by-room consultation about estate facilities and optimal haunting coordination protocols. Snort-snort. Thump. Investigative silence. Renewed snorting. "It's definitely conducting professional-quality spiritual investigation," Sarah observed with obvious fascination.

Donald felt immediate recognition that Franklin's estate consultation was being interpreted as supernatural professionalism, which suggested that Franklin's strategic abilities were generating positive attention even when filtered through ghost theory frameworks. "Very methodical spiritual presence," Donald agreed, hoping to maintain supernatural interpretation while privately planning Franklin location and retrieval strategies.

The investigation was interrupted by the discovery that Franklin had apparently identified and activated the estate's historical dumbwaiter system, a small service elevator that connected the kitchen with upper-floor guest rooms and had been designed for discrete food service delivery during the estate's Victorian social entertaining era. "The dumbwaiter's moving," Bradley observed, watching the small elevator car descend from the second floor with obvious mechanical operation.

"Ghosts operating historical estate equipment," Jessica said with obvious excitement. "This is like living in an actual supernatural movie."

Donald watched the dumbwaiter arrive at the main floor and realized that Franklin had discovered estate transportation systems that provided access to every floor of the building without using conventional stairs or hallways.

"Great-Uncle Mortimer's spiritual presence demonstrates impressive mechanical aptitude," Donald said, trying to maintain supernatural interpretation while privately admiring Franklin's creative approach to estate navigation.

The dumbwaiter opened to reveal evidence of Franklin's systematic exploration, muddy hoof prints, scattered food evidence, and what appeared to be strategic consultation notes that Franklin had somehow created through systematic arrangement of estate materials.

"The ghost is leaving documentation," Trevor said with obvious amazement.

Donald examined Franklin's "documentation" and realized that his consultation partner had been conducting comprehensive estate analysis and had organized his findings according to strategic consultation protocols that demonstrated genuine professional thoroughness.

"Great-Uncle Mortimer's spiritual consultation appears to focus on estate optimization and facility utilization efficiency," Donald observed, translating Franklin's systematic investigation into supernatural terminology.

Saturday evening's Halloween costume party was scheduled to provide the weekend's social climax, with sophisticated teenage entertainment coordination that would demonstrate appropriate family social development and age-appropriate recreational programming.

Donald had packed what he considered sophisticated costume coordination: a "Young Businessman of the Year" outfit that featured his father's best suit, professional accessories, and strategic consultation materials that would demonstrate his mature approach to teenage social development.

But when Donald arrived at the costume party, he discovered that sophisticated teenage costume coordination focused on creativity, humour, and individual personality expression rather than professional credibility and business networking demonstration. Bradley was dressed as a vampire with dramatic cape and theatrical makeup. Trevor had chosen werewolf coordination with impressive special effects and character development commitment. Jessica and Sarah had collaborated on sophisticated witch costumes that demonstrated both creative coordination and impressive attention to visual detail.

"Donald," Jessica said, examining his business costume with obvious confusion, "are you supposed to be someone specific, or just... a businessman?"

Donald felt immediate recognition that his costume strategy had missed the sophisticated creative expectations of teenage Halloween programming.

"Young entrepreneurial leadership," Donald replied, trying to present his business costume as character development rather than just professional clothing coordination.

"That's... interesting," Sarah said diplomatically.

Donald realized that his costume approach had failed to generate the kind of sophisticated social attention he'd hoped for, and that sophisticated teenage Halloween programming required creative personality expression rather than professional credibility demonstration.

The costume party atmosphere was further enhanced by renewed supernatural phenomena that provided entertainment coordination beyond anything Aunt Millicent had planned for weekend programming.

Franklin's dumbwaiter transportation system allowed him to appear in different rooms throughout the evening, creating systematic supernatural encounters that fascinated party participants and convinced adults that the estate was experiencing comprehensive spiritual visitation.

"The ghost appears to be attending our costume party," Bradley observed during one of Franklin's brief appearances via dumbwaiter transportation.

"Very social spiritual presence," Jessica added. "Great-Uncle Mortimer clearly appreciates sophisticated teenage entertainment coordination."

Donald felt immediate recognition that Franklin was providing more successful party entertainment than his own costume and conversation coordination, which meant his consultation partner was inadvertently dominating sophisticated social programming while remaining mysteriously concealed.

The evening's social climax came when the sophisticated teenage party participants decided to conduct direct supernatural communication attempts through organized séance coordination that would facilitate authentic spiritual contact with Great-Uncle Mortimer's increasingly active presence.

"Séances are classic Halloween entertainment," Sarah explained as the party participants organized around a table with candles and what appeared to be systematic spiritual communication protocols.

"Sophisticated teenagers coordinate direct supernatural investigation rather than just observing mysterious phenomena," Jessica added. Donald felt immediate panic about séance activities that could potentially result in Franklin's direct discovery and supernatural explanation compromise.

"Maybe séances require specialized equipment or professional spiritual consultation supervision?" Donald suggested desperately. "We've got candles, positive spiritual energy, and genuine curiosity about supernatural communication," Bradley replied. "That's everything you need for authentic spiritual contact."

The séance coordination proceeded with sophisticated teenage enthusiasm and what appeared to be genuine commitment to supernatural communication protocols, while Franklin's exploration activities continued to provide mysterious phenomena that convinced party participants they were experiencing authentic spiritual contact.

"Great-Uncle Mortimer," Sarah addressed the mysterious estate presence with serious spiritual communication commitment, "if you're here with us, please provide a sign of your spiritual presence." Franklin's response was immediate and unmistakable: systematic honking from the dumbwaiter system that suggested genuine supernatural communication acknowledgment.

"He's responding!" Jessica exclaimed with obvious excitement. "Direct spiritual communication confirmation," Trevor added with obvious admiration for their séance coordination effectiveness. Donald watched his sophisticated relatives and their teenage guests develop authentic excitement about supernatural communication that was actually Franklin responding to his name being mentioned during estate consultation activities.

"Great-Uncle Mortimer," Bradley continued the spiritual communication session, "can you provide additional spiritual presence demonstration for our Halloween entertainment coordination?"

Franklin's response exceeded everyone's supernatural communication expectations.

Franklin emerged from the dumbwaiter system during the middle of the séance with timing that suggested either supernatural manifestation or pig-level understanding of dramatic presentation opportunities.

But Franklin's emergence was complicated by the fact that he'd somehow acquired what appeared to be a vintage costume mask during his estate exploration activities, specifically, a theatrical mask that created the impression of supernatural presence coordination rather than standard pig appearance.

"GREAT-UNCLE MORTIMER HAS MANIFESTED!" Uncle Reginald shouted from the parlour doorway, where he'd been observing the teenage séance activities with parental supervision concern.

Franklin, apparently understanding that he was being mistaken for supernatural phenomena, honked dramatically and performed his sitting trick while wearing the theatrical mask that suggested sophisticated spiritual presence rather than neighbourhood consultation pig.

The estate's Halloween party erupted into controlled chaos, with adults documenting supernatural manifestation while sophisticated teenage party participants competed to provide direct spiritual communication with what they believed was authentic ghost presence.

"Great-Uncle Mortimer!" Aunt Millicent addressed Franklin with obvious spiritual respect. "We're honoured by your Halloween visitation! Please accept our appreciation for your supernatural entertainment coordination!"

Franklin honked acknowledgment and continued performing his consultation trick sitting while maintaining theatrical mask presentation that suggested genuine supernatural presence rather than concealed pig consultation.

Donald watched his consultation partner receive sophisticated family recognition for spiritual presence coordination and realized that Franklin had accidentally achieved the kind of sophisticated social success that Donald had been strategically planning all weekend.

"That's the most impressive supernatural manifestation I've ever witnessed," Jessica told Donald with obvious excitement and what appeared to be genuine romantic interest in his proximity to authentic spiritual phenomena.

"Great-Uncle Mortimer clearly appreciates sophisticated teenage spiritual communication," Donald replied, though he was privately amazed by Franklin's natural understanding of dramatic presentation and supernatural entertainment coordination.

The Halloween party continued with Franklin providing ongoing supernatural entertainment while maintaining theatrical mask concealment that preserved his spiritual presence interpretation and prevented pig-related explanation complications.

"Donald," Sarah said during a quiet moment between supernatural phenomena demonstrations, "you seem very comfortable with spiritual communication. Have you had experience with supernatural consultation before?"

Donald felt immediate opportunity to demonstrate sophisticated spiritual understanding without revealing Franklin's actual consultation partnership.

"I've been developing strategic consultation expertise that includes spiritual communication protocols and supernatural phenomenon analysis," Donald said, using professional terminology that suggested advanced spiritual capabilities.

"That's incredibly sophisticated," Sarah replied with obvious admiration. "Most teenagers don't understand supernatural strategic thinking."

Donald felt the kind of social recognition he'd been seeking all weekend, though the recognition was based on spiritual consultation expertise rather than business networking capabilities.

The weekend's romantic coordination reached its climax during Sunday evening's farewell activities, when sophisticated teenage programming created optimal social interaction opportunities that Donald finally understood were designed for proximity development and whatever evolved naturally from proximity development.

"Donald," Jessica said during the farewell party's quiet conversation period, "this weekend has been amazing. Great-Uncle Mortimer's spiritual presence created the most entertaining Halloween programming ever, and you seem to understand supernatural phenomena better than anyone else here."

Donald felt the kind of social success he'd been strategically planning, though the success was based on Franklin's supernatural entertainment rather than Donald's business consultation expertise.

"Spiritual consultation requires individual attention and authentic communication," Donald replied, using Franklin's relationship principles to explain supernatural communication effectiveness. "You're really good at individual attention," Jessica said, moving closer to Donald in a way that suggested sophisticated romantic coordination was developing naturally from spiritual consultation conversation.

Donald felt immediate recognition that sophisticated teenage romantic activities were finally progressing according to weekend social objectives, though the progression was happening because of Franklin's supernatural entertainment rather than Donald's strategic planning.

"Maybe we could continue spiritual consultation conversation in a more private setting?" Jessica suggested, using sophisticated teenage romantic coordination terminology that Donald finally understood meant she was interested in proximity development and whatever might evolve from proximity development.

Donald felt the kind of social confidence that came from sophisticated female romantic interest, though he was privately aware that Jessica's interest was based on his apparent supernatural consultation abilities rather than his actual business strategic planning expertise.

"I'd be honoured to provide continued spiritual consultation," Donald said, though he had no idea what continued spiritual consultation involved in sophisticated romantic coordination contexts.

Jessica led Donald toward a quieter area of the conservatory while Franklin continued providing supernatural entertainment for the remaining party participants through systematic dumbwaiter appearances and theatrical mask coordination.

"Donald," Jessica said as they settled into private conversation positioning, "I've never met anyone who understands supernatural phenomena the way you do. It's very attractive when someone has special knowledge about mysterious things."

Donald felt immediate recognition that sophisticated romantic success was finally developing, though he was completely unprepared for proximity development and whatever might evolve naturally from proximity development.

"Spiritual consultation requires authentic attention and genuine communication," Donald replied, using Franklin's relationship principles because they were the only relationship expertise he actually possessed.

"Show me," Jessica said, moving even closer to Donald in a way that clearly indicated sophisticated romantic coordination expectations. Donald felt immediate panic. Jessica was clearly expecting him to demonstrate spiritual consultation abilities through romantic interaction, but Donald's spiritual consultation expertise consisted entirely of watching Franklin provide therapeutic support to neighbourhood children and community service collaboration.

"Spiritual consultation focuses on individual attention and authentic care," Donald said uncertainly, though he was beginning to realize that romantic coordination involved different kinds of individual attention than Franklin's therapeutic consultation approaches.
"I like individual attention," Jessica said, clearly expecting Donald to provide romantic coordination that demonstrated his spiritual consultation capabilities.

Donald was attempting to figure out how spiritual consultation translated into romantic interaction when Franklin's weekend entertainment reached its most spectacular climax.

The estate's wine cellar had apparently been Franklin's strategic objective all weekend. While adults focused on supernatural phenomena investigation and sophisticated teenagers pursued romantic coordination activities, Franklin had been conducting systematic exploration that culminated in comprehensive wine cellar consultation.

Franklin's wine cellar investigation had several unintended consequences. First, Franklin had accidentally knocked over multiple wine bottles during his systematic exploration, creating acoustic phenomena that exceeded previous supernatural entertainment levels. Second, Franklin had somehow acquired additional costume elements during his wine cellar consultation, specifically, a vintage cape that enhanced his theatrical presence coordination. Third, Franklin had attracted the attention of other sophisticated teenage party participants who'd been planning their own wine cellar access activities.

"WHAT IS THAT?" Bradley's voice carried from the direction of the wine cellar with obvious alarm and confusion.
Donald felt immediate panic about Franklin discovery and supernatural explanation compromise.

"Maybe Great-Uncle Mortimer is conducting spiritual wine inventory?" Donald suggested desperately, though he was privately calculating emergency Franklin retrieval and damage control strategies.

"Let's investigate," Jessica said with obvious excitement about direct supernatural encounter opportunities.

Donald followed Jessica toward the wine cellar while developing emergency strategic plans for Franklin situation management that would preserve both his consultation partner's supernatural interpretation and his own weekend romantic coordination success. The wine cellar investigation revealed Franklin at the height of his supernatural entertainment career. He was wearing his acquired theatrical mask and vintage cape while systematically investigating wine bottle arrangements, occasionally honking supernatural responses to his own exploration activities, and generally conducting himself with the dignity appropriate for sophisticated spiritual presence coordination.

"GREAT-UNCLE MORTIMER!" Uncle Reginald announced with obvious spiritual recognition enthusiasm.

Franklin looked up from his wine investigation, honked official supernatural acknowledgment, and performed his sitting trick while maintaining full theatrical costume coordination.

"He's magnificent," Jessica said with obvious spiritual phenomena appreciation.

"Most impressive supernatural manifestation I've ever witnessed," Sarah added.

Donald watched Franklin receive sophisticated family recognition for spiritual presence while maintaining theatrical concealment that preserved supernatural interpretation and prevented pig-related explanation complications.

But Franklin's wine cellar supernatural entertainment was complicated by the arrival of additional sophisticated teenage party participants who'd been planning independent wine access activities and were unprepared for supernatural presence coordination during their alcohol procurement efforts.

"Oh my God," one of the arriving teenagers said, clearly unprepared for Franklin's theatrical spiritual presence.
"The ghost is real," another added with obvious supernatural recognition and alcohol-influenced enthusiasm.

Franklin, surrounded by sophisticated teenage audiences and sophisticated adult spiritual recognition, apparently decided that comprehensive supernatural entertainment required expanded performance coordination.

Franklin began conducting what appeared to be systematic spiritual consultation for all assembled family members and party participants, providing supernatural honking responses to questions about estate history, spiritual presence protocols, and optimal Halloween entertainment coordination.

"Great-Uncle Mortimer is providing spiritual consultation," Aunt Millicent observed with obvious supernatural appreciation.
"Advanced spiritual intelligence and comprehensive ghostly social coordination," Uncle Reginald added.

Donald watched Franklin provide supernatural consultation that demonstrated all his authentic therapeutic abilities while maintaining theatrical presentation that suggested spiritual presence rather than pig consultation partnership.

"Donald," Jessica said quietly during Franklin's supernatural consultation performance, "you really understand how to communicate with spiritual phenomena. That's incredibly sophisticated."

Donald felt the kind of romantic recognition he'd been strategically planning all weekend, though the recognition was based on Franklin's supernatural entertainment rather than Donald's business networking capabilities.

"Spiritual consultation requires authentic attention and genuine communication," Donald replied, using Franklin's relationship principles because they were the only supernatural expertise he actually possessed.

"You're very good at authentic attention," Jessica said, clearly indicating that romantic coordination was progressing according to sophisticated teenage social development objectives.

Donald felt immediate confidence about romantic success combined with panic about Franklin discovery and supernatural explanation maintenance requirements.

Sunday morning brought the weekend's most challenging strategic crisis when Franklin's supernatural entertainment generated attention that exceeded estate family programming and attracted professional supernatural investigation services.

"We've called the Society for Psychical Research," Aunt Millicent announced during Sunday breakfast. "Professional supernatural investigators who specialize in authentic spiritual phenomena documentation and ghostly presence verification."

Donald felt immediate panic about professional supernatural investigation that could potentially result in Franklin discovery and pig-related explanation requirements that would compromise both his consultation partner's safety and his own weekend social success.

"Professional supernatural investigators?" Donald asked, trying to assess the scope of the investigative challenge Franklin's entertainment had created.

"Experts in spiritual presence documentation and ghostly communication protocols," Uncle Reginald explained. "They're driving up from the city this afternoon to conduct comprehensive supernatural consultation about Great-Uncle Mortimer's increasingly active spiritual presence."

Donald realized that Franklin's successful supernatural entertainment had generated professional attention that exceeded anything Donald could manage through strategic planning or damage control coordination.

"Franklin," Donald said quietly during his private consultation session with his concealed partner, "professional supernatural investigators are going to require more sophisticated spiritual presence coordination than theatrical mask and costume presentation."

Franklin honked thoughtful acknowledgment and looked at Donald with obvious concern about expanded performance requirements. "The thing is," Donald continued, "you've been providing genuine consultation and authentic attention all weekend. Everyone loves Great-Uncle Mortimer because you've been using your real consultation abilities to make people feel valued and entertained." Franklin performed his sitting trick and honked what sounded like understanding about authentic consultation versus performance presentation.

"Maybe," Donald said, "instead of trying to maintain supernatural explanation, we should just introduce you as yourself and let people appreciate your actual consultation abilities?"

Franklin honked enthusiastic agreement and began removing his theatrical costume coordination, apparently ready to provide consultation services as authentic Franklin rather than supernatural Great-Uncle Mortimer.

Sunday afternoon's professional supernatural investigation provided the perfect opportunity for Franklin's authentic consultation debut with sophisticated family audiences who'd been appreciating his abilities all weekend without understanding their actual source.

"Before the professional investigators arrive," Donald announced to the assembled family members and sophisticated teenage guests, "I have a confession about Great-Uncle Mortimer's spiritual presence." Donald felt the kind of strategic clarity that came from understanding authentic relationship priorities rather than competitive positioning objectives.

"Great-Uncle Mortimer's spiritual presence," Donald continued, "is actually my consultation partner Franklin Roosevelt, who's been providing strategic estate exploration and supernatural entertainment coordination throughout the weekend."

Franklin emerged from concealment with his characteristic dignity and performed his sitting trick for the assembled audience, clearly demonstrating his authentic consultation abilities rather than supernatural phenomena.

"A pig," Uncle Reginald said slowly. "Great-Uncle Mortimer's spiritual presence is actually a pig."

"Franklin Roosevelt," Donald confirmed. "Strategic consultation specialist and therapeutic support provider who's been offering individual attention and authentic care to everyone who appreciated Great-Uncle Mortimer's spiritual consultation."

The sophisticated family audience considered this revelation while Franklin honked politely and offered his hoof for formal introduction to relatives who'd been appreciating his abilities all weekend without understanding their actual source.

"That's the most intelligent pig I've ever encountered," Aunt Millicent said, accepting Franklin's hoof shake with obvious respect for his demonstrated consultation capabilities.

"And the most entertaining supernatural phenomena we've ever experienced," Uncle Reginald added. "Franklin's consultation abilities exceed anything Great-Uncle Mortimer ever provided during his actual lifetime."

Donald felt the kind of family recognition that came from authentic relationship development rather than competitive strategic positioning.

"Franklin," Jessica said, approaching the pig with obvious appreciation, "you provided better spiritual consultation than any actual ghost could have managed. Your individual attention made everyone feel genuinely valued and entertained."

Franklin honked acknowledgment and performed his sitting trick specifically for Jessica, clearly demonstrating the authentic consultation abilities that had generated sophisticated social recognition throughout the weekend.

Sunday evening's farewell activities confirmed that Franklin's authentic consultation abilities had generated family appreciation and sophisticated teenage social recognition that exceeded anything Donald could have achieved through strategic networking or business demonstration.

"Donald," Aunt Millicent said as the family prepared for departure, "Franklin's consultation capabilities demonstrate impressive strategic intelligence and genuine social coordination abilities. You should be proud of the partnership you've developed."

"Franklin taught me that authentic relationships provide more satisfaction than competitive positioning," Donald replied. "This weekend he demonstrated that being genuinely helpful generates better social success than trying to impress people with strategic planning."

Donald felt recognition that his sophisticated relatives appreciated Franklin's authentic abilities and Donald's genuine partnership coordination rather than competitive business demonstration or strategic networking attempts.

"Plus," Bradley added with obvious respect, "Franklin created the best Halloween entertainment we've ever experienced. Much better than standard costume party programming."

"And Donald," Jessica said with obvious romantic appreciation, "your individual attention and authentic communication made this weekend really special. I hope we can continue spiritual consultation coordination when you visit the city."

Donald felt the kind of romantic success he'd been strategically planning, though the success was based on authentic relationship development rather than business networking or supernatural expertise demonstration.

As Donald and Franklin departed the estate Sunday evening, Donald felt confident that his consultation partner had demonstrated genuine social value and authentic relationship capabilities that created family recognition and sophisticated teenage appreciation.

"Franklin," Donald said during the drive home, "this weekend you proved that being authentically helpful generates better social success than any strategic positioning or competitive demonstration."

Franklin honked thoughtful agreement and settled comfortably for the journey home.

"And I learned," Donald continued, "that sophisticated relatives appreciate genuine consultation abilities and authentic individual attention more than business networking or professional credibility demonstration."

Franklin performed his sitting trick within the car's transportation space and honked what sounded like satisfaction with Donald's evolving understanding of authentic relationship priorities.

As Donald planned ongoing consultation services that would focus on genuine therapeutic support rather than business demonstration, he felt the kind of confidence that came from understanding meaningful social success.

The weekend had ended, but Donald's education in authentic relationship development and genuine consultation partnership was continuing to evolve through Franklin's natural therapeutic abilities and social intelligence.

Franklin honked goodnight as they arrived home, and Donald fell asleep planning consultation services that would help people with authentic difficulties rather than trying to impress relatives with strategic business capabilities.

He still had no idea that the most important lesson about genuine friendship was yet to come.

Printed in Dunstable, United Kingdom